D1288755

A Faithful Heart:

Preparing for the High Holy Days

A Study Text Based on the Midrash
Maaseh Avraham Avinu

Benjamin Levy

With a foreword by Rabbi Norman Cohen

UAHC PRESS
NEW YORK, NEW YORK

Library of Congress Cataloging-in-Publication Data

Levy, Benjamin, Rabbi.
　　A faithful heart: preparing for the High Holy Days: a study text based on the midrash
Ma'aseh Avraham avinu / Benjamin Levy; with foreword by Norman Cohen.
　　　　p. cm.
　　Includes the text of Ma'aseh Avraham avinu in Hebrew and English.
　　ISBN 0-8074-0754-2 (pbk.: alk. paper)
　　　1. Ma'aseh Avraham avinu. 2. Abraham (Biblical patriarch)—Legends.
　3. High Holidays. 4. Jewish religious education—Textbooks for adults. I. Ma'aseh Avraham avinu.
Enlgish & Hebrew. II. Title.

BM517.M193 2001
296.4'31—dc21

2001046145

Typesetting: El Ot Ltd., Tel Aviv
This book is printed on acid-free paper.
Copyright © 2001 by the UAHC Press
Manufactured in the United States of America
10 9 8 7 6 5 4 3 2 1

For

my wonderful wife,

Evelyn,

and two boys,

Elijah and Reuven,

fellow travelers upon the path.

"God said to Abram, 'Go forth from your country,
your place of birth, and from your father's house
to a land that I will show you.'"

Genesis 12:1

Contents

Acknowledgments

When I began working on *A Faithful Heart: Preparing for the High Holy Days* over five years ago as a student at Hebrew Union College–Jewish Institute of Religion, Rabbi Norman Cohen was there to advise, assist, and lead. From that time to this, Rabbi Cohen has consistently "been there" for me: he has counseled in times of professional upheaval, officially installed me as a pulpit rabbi, and aided me immeasurably through every step of the preparation of this present volume. The arrangement of the commentary into *p'shat* and *d'rash* sections was his idea. I am grateful not only for his expertise, but his continued friendship.

I also want to thank Rabbi Hara Person of the UAHC Press. Hara's patience with this first-time author has been much appreciated, as she guided me through the publishing process with great sensitivity. Her spiritual awareness and skilled editing have shaped and enhanced this book, including the provision of the title. Working with her over these past months has been a truly positive experience. She has taught me much. I would also like to thank other members of the Press who have helped give life to this book: Ken Gesser, Stuart Benick, Liane Broido, Rachel Gleiberman, Rick Abrams, and Debra Hirsch Corman.

I have been blessed with friends over the years who have lent not only support, but also literary advice and proofreading. I want to thank Mark Sohmer for his consistent encouragement and Tony Seideman for allowing me to approach the literary world through his sound vision and for teaching me the structure of a book proposal. I thank Jack Wertheimer for his years of support, his computer tips, and the many hours he spent reading and rereading portions of this manuscript. His suggestions have proved invaluable.

I also want to thank my study partners Rabbis Michael Arsers, Jonathan Lubliner, and Neal Gold for helping me grow in Torah and for listening to me talk about the book. I thank Rabbi Mark Bloom for allowing me to quote him and Cantor Joel Coleman for his keen eye. I thank Rabbi Niles Goldstein for fielding my phone calls with friendliness and for allowing me to benefit from his experience.

I thank my family for always coming through. I thank my parents, Deborah and Sam ע״ה, for bringing me into this world, and my brother, Ira, for his understanding. I thank my Nona Becky ע״ה for instilling a sense of Jewish identity within me. I am grateful to my Aunt Lisa for her constant caring and to my Cousins Ira and Irwin who have been big brothers. I thank Ira, an author in his own right, for reviewing portions of the text. I pay tribute to my sister, Ronda ע״ה, whose deeds of unselfish righteousness and pride in me will always be an inspiration.

Finally, I thank my wife, Evelyn, without whose love and strength I would be lost. Thank you for being my anchor. I also thank our sons, Elijah and Reuven, who give meaning to our lives by challenging us to be the best we can be.

Acknowledgments

The Vilna Gaon taught that upon experiencing every important phase and accomplishment of one's life, a person should thank the Holy One. So, it is at this opportunity that I humbly acknowledge and express gratitude to my Creator for giving me life, sustaining me, and allowing me to reach this day!

Rabbi Ben Levy

November 27, 2000
29th of Cheshvan, 5761
Monroe Township, New Jersey

Foreword

And it came to pass after these things that God put Abraham to the test. He said to him, "Abraham," and he answered, "Here I am." And He said, "Take your son, your favored one, Isaac, whom you love, and go to the land of Moriah, and offer him there as a burnt offering on one of the mountains that I will show you."

Genesis 22:1–2

Each year when we hear the story of the *Akeidah*—the Binding of Isaac—read on Rosh HaShanah, we find it incredible that Abraham agreed to God's demand that he sacrifice his son Isaac without a word of protest. How could he so cavalierly bring the son of his old age, the child for whom he and Sarah waited, to the sacrificial altar, when he, himself, had argued for the lives of the righteous at Sodom and Gemorrah?

What we overlook, however, is the fact that this was not the first time that God had tested Abraham. According to the rabbinic tradition, this indeed was the last in a series of ten tests that Abraham had undergone, which spanned the whole of Abraham's life.

The Rabbis point out in this regard that the opening words of the account of the *Akeidah* underscore this very point. Listen to the words again: "And it came to pass after these things that God put Abraham to the test." Although the phrase "And it came to pass after these things" is formulaic and should be translated as "sometime later," every reader asks, "What events preceded the *Akeidah* that gave rise to it? What things occurred that made it necessary for God to demand that Abraham sacrifice his son Isaac or prompted Abraham to agree to the command?" What preceded the test of the *Akeidah* were nine trials that Abraham had to endure. Abraham came to the final test realizing that in each of the previous tests all had worked out in the end. Therefore, he had every right to expect that somehow this tenth test would end in the same way. Isaac would live!

However, although Abraham had succeeded in passing every test that God had placed upon him, in each case God had guaranteed the outcome in one way or another. Even in banishing Hagar and Ishmael (in Genesis 21), Abraham was assured that Ishmael would become the progenitor of a great nation made up of twelve tribes, just as his half-brother Isaac. But could Abraham sacrifice Isaac, the very guarantor of the future? Would he be willing to put his son's life on the line when there was no promise that he would be spared? Indeed, all the promises and guarantees of the past were now doomed, since they depended on Isaac's survival. On Mount Moriah, God would learn just how deep was Abraham's faith.

Yet even from his childhood, Abraham's great faith was evident to God. The midrash *Maaseh Avraham Avinu,* which explores the early life of Abraham, providing the reasons why God chose him to be the first Jew, emphasizes Abraham's faithfulness. Living in a world suffused with idolatry, Abraham stands alone as the person of faith, the only one who believes in the one God of the universe. As framed by the author of this wonderful translation, commentary, and study guide, *Maaseh Avraham Avinu* is made up of a series of tests that demonstrate Abraham's character. Whether it be his miraculous survival after his birth, his confrontation with King Nimrod, or his emergence from the fiery furnace, Abraham meets every ordeal and grows in his faith and in his capacity for righteousness.

Rabbi Ben Levy's *A Faithful Heart* is a user-friendly rendition of *Maaseh Avraham Avinu.* It is a valuable tool for High Holy Day preparation because it underscores many of the key themes of Rosh HaShanah and Yom Kippur. However, its significance for our lives goes far beyond the meaningfulness of the Days of Awe. Like Abraham, each of us experiences many different kinds of challenges in our lives. *Maaseh Avraham Avinu,* through this creative rendition, forces us to reflect continually about our own trials and how we have handled them. None of us goes through life without facing difficulties personally, as members of families, or as participants in communities. The only effective questions are "How do we handle our tests of faith?" and "Have they led to personal growth and a deepening of our commitment to live with wise purpose?"

In reading *A Faithful Heart,* each of us will be challenged not simply to imbibe the power of this intriguing rabbinic story of Abraham's childhood, but to struggle with ourselves—who we are and who we can become. May we, the progeny of Abraham, grow in our faith, our Jewish commitment, and our humanity as we enjoy this immersion into the fanciful world of rabbinic midrash.

Rabbi Norman J. Cohen
Acting President
Hebrew Union College–
Jewish Institute of Religion

INTRODUCTION

Preparation for the Days of Awe

The Hebrew calendar confronts us with the challenge of preprogrammed time designed to encompass a full range of human emotion and experience. As such, the lexicon provides a year replete with highs and lows, holy days and nights, celebrations and fasts, and times of renewal. Although our ultimate goal is to sanctify all the moments of life, our Torah clearly indicates that there are some days that may be regarded as specific high points of the year. These are the מוֹעֲדִים (mo-adim), the "set times" of the year, our temporal "meeting places" with God. The Days of Awe, or High Holy Days as they are colloquially known, qualify as prime examples of such times.

While the Torah ordains the High Holy Days and the calendar on the wall confirms their dates, to fully benefit from the experience of these days requires effort from us. To travel the spiritual path from the low point of the year, Tishah B'Av (a fast day of mourning, the ninth day of the month of Av), to the high of Rosh HaShanah within the space of seven weeks indicates that we must build toward our goal. To fully immerse ourselves in the High Holy Day process, and grow as a result, means preparation. This preparation may take a number of forms. Prayer, study, self-examination, repentance, and restitution for past mistakes can all be considered steps to our goal.

Traditionally, this preparation has been reflected in our lectionary's "seven haftarot of consolation," Isaiah's messages of comfort and renewal; the weekly study of *Pirkei Avot*, the Mishnaic compendium of ethical behavior; and *S'lichot*, prayer services aimed toward seeking God's forgiveness for our having missed the mark during the past year. However, there is an additional tradition indicated by two of the manuscripts used to prepare this volume. These documents present *Maaseh Avraham Avinu*, a sixteenth-century midrashic study text used by Jews to prepare for and to immerse themselves in the High Holy Day experience. In fact, the Valmadonna Trust Library's manuscript 167 lists *Maaseh Avraham Avinu* as a *Tikkun Leil Rosh HaShanah*, a text that may be studied on the first evening of Rosh HaShanah.

Maaseh Avraham Avinu proves to be so valuable a tool for High Holy Day preparation because it connects to the Days of Awe in three basic ways. First, the midrash beautifully illustrates the various themes associated with the High Holy Day season. Second, it alludes to and provides insight into the scriptural readings of the holidays, most notably the *Akeidah* (the Binding of Isaac), read on Rosh HaShanah, and the Book of Jonah, read on Yom Kippur. Third, the text contains contextual and linguistic references to the High Holy Day liturgy.

High Holy Day Themes

Maaseh Avraham Avinu illustrates a number of High Holy Day themes. In focusing upon the theme of God's unity, the midrash features the notion of God as Creator. This proves particularly appropriate to Rosh HaShanah, since this holiday is traditionally regarded as the world's birthday, the anniversary of Creation. That God is also the "Sovereign of sovereigns" is an oft-repeated declaration throughout the midrash. This again is a major theme of Rosh HaShanah, the holiday that celebrates, in effect, the annual recoronation of God.

God's sovereignty is reflected in *Maaseh Avraham Avinu* by the ability to judge fairly and mete out consequences. God sees the merit of Abraham's righteousness and loyalty and saves him time and again from the clutches of King Nimrod, the evil despot who rules the world through deceit, violence, and idolatry. Thus, God repeatedly defeats the designs of the earthly monarch, proving that Nimrod's power is no match for that of the Master of the universe. Divine justice relates to the High Holy Days because, according to tradition, on Rosh HaShanah God judges every living creature and determines its fate for the following year. According to legend, the heavenly decree is written on the New Year and sealed on Yom Kippur. The days in between may be spent in repentance and acts of righteousness in order to tip the scale of justice in one's favor, so that one's fate for the coming year may be changed for the better.

Maaseh Avraham Avinu depicts the human need for spiritual experience in that it presents Abraham's quest for God in his life. During the High Holy Days especially, we search for God in our lives. In fact, the Days of Awe may be entitled as such because our perception of and concentration upon God's presence engenders these days with a sense of awe.

The midrash also reveals the power of repentance or *t'shuvah,* the ability to turn back to God and to goodness, to return to that image of our higher selves. It reminds us that we are not destined to repeat the same mistakes over and over again. Rather, people can change. We are all capable of growth, regardless of age or past mistakes. *T'shuvah* is one of the major themes and goals of the High Holy Days, so much so that the period is also known as the עֲשֶׂרֶת יְמֵי תְּשׁוּבָה (*Aseret Y'mei T'shuvah*), "the Ten Days of *T'shuvah.*"

Maaseh Avraham Avinu also reminds us of the efficacy of prayer and good intentions. In this midrash, God, who knows all, responds to Abraham's prayers for help and turns to the Patriarch in mercy upon perception of his good intentions. Certainly, prayer shines through as one of the primary themes and activities of the High Holy Days. The prayer services on these holy days are the most comprehensive of the year. The midrash challenges us to acknowledge that prayer can serve as an essential part of our process of growth by helping us get in touch with the Holy One, the God of the heaven and the earth (the transcendent and immanent Divine Presence).

The story of Abraham as related by *Maaseh Avraham Avinu* models what it means to be God's servant. The tale shows that dedication to God's goodness, living a righteous life, is not without its trials and challenges. In the midrash, Abraham not only displays the courage and conviction to withstand every trial, but actually comes to utilize each test as a tool for spiritual and personal growth so that he may continue to spread God's morality in the world.

We too are no strangers to trials and challenges in our lives and in our world. The High Holy Day process of introspection and soul-searching is one that helps provide perspective so that we, like our Patriarch Abraham, may utilize these experiences for self-improvement, to elevate our selves in holiness and service for the good. The Days of Awe may be seen as a critical period in the task of redoubling our efforts to bring God's redemption to a broken world. We, like Abraham, are God's representatives on earth. God's influence for the good in this world can depend upon our ability and our willingness to adapt the behaviors that Abraham models: courage, conviction, perseverance, faith, kindness, open-mindedness, love, and humility.

High Holy Day Scriptural Readings

In addition to the thematic references to the High Holy Days inherent in the text of *Maaseh Avraham Avinu,* we also find motifs and verbal hints related to the lectionary of the Days of Awe. For instance, the phrase "the two of them went off together," found in the midrash (3:60–61) in relation to Abraham and his father, Terach, is also featured in the Genesis account of the *Akeidah* (the Binding of Isaac, one of the Torah readings for Rosh HaShanah) in relation to Abraham and his son, Isaac (Genesis 22:6, 8). The scene in the midrash in which Abraham is bound and about to be thrown into the fiery furnace not only reflects, but offers insight into the *Akeidah. Maaseh Avraham Avinu* helps us understand that Abraham knows full well what it's like to be bound and how to face sacrifice with a faithful heart for "the sanctification of God's name." By bringing Isaac up to the mountain, Abraham is only teaching his beloved son to follow in his footsteps. The two of them truly "went off together," in more ways than one.

Maaseh Avraham Avinu also alludes, in a similar way, to Genesis 21, the story of the banishment of Hagar and Ishmael, traditionally the scriptural reading for the first day of the New Year. The events the midrash chronicles of Abraham's infancy, the mortal dangers he is exposed to, and the divine redemption that is realized, all parallel the story of Ishmael. Again, in putting Hagar and Ishmael through the ordeal of exile in the wilderness and having to demonstrate faith in God's ability to save, Abraham is only providing them an experience that he himself has already lived through. This motif also prefigures the path of the Jewish people, who will be exiled and will experience God's redemption in the wilderness.

The Book of Jonah serves as the haftarah for the afternoon of Yom Kippur. *Maaseh Avraham Avinu* contains thematic parallels that remind the reader of the haftarah. The theme of attempting to flee from God's presence appears both in Jonah and in the midrash. In both instances, the personalities depicted in the text realize the impossibility of such a quest. God is indeed everywhere. Despite efforts to the contrary, we cannot go where God is not. We neither happily shed our identities as Jews, nor shirk our mission to work for God's goodness in the world.

The motif of the prophet entering the city of his enemy and preaching the word of God proves characteristic of both *Maaseh Avraham Avinu* and Jonah. In the latter, Jonah enters Nineveh, the capital of the Assyrians, to deliver God's message of *t'shuvah* in the streets and marketplaces. In the midrash, Abraham goes to Nimrod's capital, Babylonia, to relate the message of God's reality in the streets and marketplaces. In both instances, the people respond favorably. In the Book of Jonah, the people repent their evil ways, adopt righteous behaviors, and thereby avert the divine decree to overthrow the city. In *Maaseh Avraham Avinu* more and more people abandon their idolatrous beliefs and sinful behaviors to profess faith in the One God, the God of righteousness, a trend that eventually leads to the changing of Nimrod's fiery furnace of destruction into a garden of tranquility and utopian splendor. This motif indicates to the reader that, despite our feelings of alienation and thoughts of inadequacy, our actions and efforts for the good can be surprisingly effective in changing the world around us.

High Holy Day Liturgy

Maaseh Avraham Avinu makes use of the motifs and language of the High Holy Day liturgy. For instance, the midrash contains allusions to parts of the *Aleinu* prayer (originally composed for the Rosh HaShanah Shofar Service), such as "You are our God; there is none else" and "The Eternal One is God in the heavens above and on the earth below; there is none else." In addition, the midrash mirrors the flow of the prayer. That is, in the beginning of the prayer we attest to our devotion to God (by bowing down) and to our minority status as Jews, for whom the Creator has seen fit to provide a lot that differs from that of the multitudes. Similarly, in the beginning of the midrash, Abraham finds himself an outnumbered minority in terms of his dedication to the One God.

The *Aleinu* prayer ends in anticipation of the day when our actions of healing the world will culminate in the day when "the Eternal shall be One, and God's name shall be One." *Maaseh Avraham Avinu* concludes with Abraham having turned the tables on Nimrod. Whereas at one time Abraham stood as the lone figure dedicated to the One God opposing the evils of the idolatrous king, now Nimrod remains the only one on the idolatrous side of the equation. Abraham's efforts literally bear fruit, as the fiery furnace of idolatrous destruction is transformed into a peaceful garden, with its wood flowering and giving fruit, a symbol of divine redemption.

The midrash's use of the word תּוֹקֶף *(tokef)*, which means "power," points to the *Un'taneh Tokef* prayer of the High Holy Day liturgy. While the prayer speaks of the awesome power of the judgment days of Rosh HaShanah and Yom Kippur and of the positive influence of *t'filah, t'shuvah,* and *tzedakah* (prayer, repentance, and righteousness) in our lives, the midrash uses the term ironically, even mockingly, to describe Nimrod's intention to have others worship him as a god as a result of the "power" he will display by throwing a drunken feast. To the Jewish reader, this is a reminder about what and whom is truly "powerful" in life.

Maaseh Avraham Avinu also features the phrase "The Eternal, He is God." Originally found in I Kings 18:39, the triumphant denouement in the story of Elijah's contest versus the priests of Baal on Mount Carmel, this phrase constitutes the final word of the High Holy Day liturgy, uttered at the closing moments of Yom Kippur. Its inclusion in the midrash connects the reader to that dramatic liturgical moment.

Finally, on these High Holy Days, we stand before God, not only as individuals, but as members of the Jewish people, people of the received tradition of Judaism. The phrase "the Maggid said," which appears repeatedly in the midrash, points to this received tradition, as do the stories of Abraham, the first link in this great chain of tradition.

Part of the High Holy Day liturgy beseeches God to deal mercifully with us for the sake of the merit of the Patriarchs, of whom Abraham was the first. "Remember the kind deeds of Abraham, let his righteousness plead for us..." are the words of a Rosh HaShanah *piyut* (liturgical poem). The same *piyut* alludes to Psalm 18:31, "The word of the Eternal is tried." *Midrash T'hillim* to Psalm 18 teaches that this verse refers to Abraham and the ten trials he underwent for the word of the Eternal. The first trial, *Midrash T'hillim* informs, took place in the fiery furnace, the episode that constitutes the culmination and essence of *Maaseh Avraham Avinu*.

Thus, the midrash not only reflects the themes and language of the High Holy Day liturgy, but bears a more direct connection. A segment of our prayers for the Days of Awe actually alludes to the central event of *Maaseh Avraham Avinu*, the trial of the fiery furnace. Hence, the midrash may be seen as woven into the very fabric of our worship on these very special days.

History and Structure of the Text

The term "midrash" comes from the Hebrew verb לִדְרוֹשׁ (*lidrosh*), to "draw out" or "investigate." Midrash, then, is rabbinic literature that seeks to extract and explicate the relevance of biblical text by filling in "between the lines." For instance, by the time the Torah introduces God's initiation of Abraham's mission with the words "Go forth!" the Patriarch is already seventy-five years old. The biblical text never explicitly states why God chooses Abraham to be the first Jew. Nor does the Torah provide any substantial information as to Abraham's life prior to the three-quarter century mark that may have influenced God's decision (and informed our understanding).

Maaseh Avraham Avinu helps fill in the missing information. The midrash explores the early life of Abraham. The text illustrates those personality traits and accomplishments of Abraham that cause God and the rest of humankind to take notice. In doing so, the piece explains why Abraham is still a relevant role model for us today.

Although *Maaseh Avraham Avinu* clearly makes use of ancient exegetic midrashic source materials (such as *Pirkei D'Rabbi Eliezer* and *B'reishit Rabbah*) and neatly weaves them into a biblical-style narrative, the origins of the piece remain obscure. The Constantinople edition constitutes the earliest recorded appearance of the midrash. According to some, this edition was published in 1519, while others insist upon 1580. Regardless of the exact date of this first printed edition, in the opinion of Rabbi Norman Cohen, one may assume an earlier manuscript tradition in regard to the midrash's origin.

Four printed editions (including the Constantinople pressing) and four manuscripts of *Maaseh Avraham Avinu* remain available today. All eight extant editions have been used to prepare the Hebrew text as it appears in this volume. The translation and commentaries have been provided by myself.

The commentary is dual in nature, divided into *p'shat* and *d'rash*. *P'shat,* or "simple meaning," provides information that is essential to the reader for an immediate, straightforward understanding of the story. The *d'rash* section challenges the reader to identify formulaic and thematic parallels, not only from biblical and rabbinic literatures, but from his or her own life. The commentary is supported by a section of gleanings and explanatory essays, which appear at the conclusion of each chapter of text. A short essay introduces each new episode.

The midrash itself is structured so that it may be seen as two halves of four major episodes each (three episodes to a half appear in this volume). The first half of *Maaseh Avraham Avinu* concerns the life of Abraham from before conception through the first month of his life. The second half depicts the Patriarch at twenty years of age.

Each episode represents another test for Abraham. Every time, as one might expect, Abraham not only proves equal to the challenge, but manages somehow to use the ordeal to grow in faith and good deeds. Each chapter, then, begins with a challenge and concludes with praise of God. Both halves culminate in direct confrontations between the evil tyrant King Nimrod and Abraham. The Patriarch, as God's representative, consistently wins these confrontations. At the beginning of the midrash, Abraham stands alone in an idolatrous, immoral world as the only believer in and practitioner of true religion. By the story's denouement, Nimrod remains the only idolater.

As mentioned above, the midrash as prepared for this volume has been trimmed to include only three episodes to a half. The edited material has been summarized in the short essays that introduce each chapter, so the flow of the tale remains smooth and complete.

The text provided here is thus divided into six essential chapters, lending itself to study as a preparation for the High Holy Days in much the same manner as *Pirkei Avot* (which also has six chapters)—a chapter a week, from the second Sabbath subsequent to Tishah B'Av through the month of Elul. Just as the object of learning *Pirkei Avot* remains the translation of its wisdom into deeds of mitzvah, so too can the study of *Maaseh Avraham Avinu* lead us to the performance of the acts of kindness and righteousness that elevate us as human beings and define us as Jews.

MAASEH AVRAHAM AVINU

Chapter 1

God's Uniqueness: A Miraculous Birth, Physical Survival

The story opens with the depiction of an idolatrous, immoral world ruled by King Nimrod, originally mentioned in Genesis 10:9 as a "mighty hunter." Nimrod exalts himself as a god. The people of his era serve and worship him.

Nimrod, a skilled astrologer, predicts that a boy will be born who will usurp the king's faith. By means of a royal decree, Nimrod murders seventy thousand infants to prevent this.

When the angels on high witness this rampant slaughter, they ask God whether the Holy One is aware of the evil that has occurred. God replies in the affirmative and assures that not only does God see, but they soon will see how the power of the Divine will be used to administer justice vis-à-vis Nimrod.

Thus, the midrash sets the stage for a contest that pits God's might versus earthly (tyrannical) power. The text presents Abraham's birth as the first chapter in this struggle, as Nimrod's murderous decree places the future Patriarch's very existence in immediate peril.

In this way, Abraham's emergence serves as a metaphor for the birth of all positive turns in life in which the initial hours prove critical. Success is dependent not just on the actions of humans but also on divine help. This is true in terms of both physical and spiritual survival. Whether major surgery is successful often is apparent only after the passing of forty-eight hours. In such a case, the doctors do all they can do, but a positive outcome ultimately depends upon the realm beyond that of human hands.

In the spiritual sphere, the survival of the "new selves" we create through our sincere participation in the High Holy Day process also hangs in the balance during their early hours. Just as Nimrod seeks to destroy the baby Abraham, many factors may conspire to annihilate our "reborn" selves before they can establish a positive pattern for our lives and the lives of those around us. Our turning to God in these critical hours can provide strength.

Both of these aspects, physical and spiritual survival, tie Abraham's birth to the themes of the High Holy Day period. Regarded as the anniversary of the creation of human life on earth, Abraham's birth may be seen as a new chapter in the ongoing process of Creation. Just as God creates the physical world, so too does God create the spiritual-moral universe by inspiring human beings to help spread the message of divine kindness.

In addition, Abraham's struggle to survive points to the Jewish tradition regarding these Days of Awe as a time to contemplate our mortality. It is this consideration of our ultimate limitation that gives rise to the great questions of purpose in life, for which spiritual values and faith in God can help spell the answer.

1:1	The Maggid said that at that time	אָמַר הַמַּגִּיד שֶׁבְּזְמַן הַהוּא
	the mother of Abraham, our patriarch	הָלְכָה אֵם אַבְרָהָם אָבִינוּ,
1:3	may he rest in peace, went and	עָלָיו הַשָּׁלוֹם,
	married a man named Terach,	וְלָקְחָה אִישׁ תֶּרַח שְׁמוֹ
1:5	and conceived with him. At	וְתַהַר מִמֶּנּוּ. וַיְהִי
	about the third month,	כְּמִשְׁלֹשׁ חֳדָשִׁים
1:7	her belly became enlarged	וַתִּגְדַּל בִּטְנָהּ
	and her face grew pale.	וּפָנֶיהָ מוֹרִיקוֹת.
1:9	Terach, her husband, said to her,	אָמַר לָהּ תֶּרַח בַּעֲלָהּ,
	"What's the matter with you, my wife?	"מַה לָךְ אִשְׁתִּי,
1:11	Your face is pale	פָּנַיִךְ מוֹרִיקוֹת
	and your belly enlarged."	וּבִטְנֵךְ גְדוֹלָה?"

P'shat: 1:1. The Maggid said. The "Maggid," or storyteller, appears from time to time throughout *Maaseh Avraham Avinu* as a narrator who provides useful information that pushes the story forward. **1:6. third month.** Pregnancy generally becomes noticeable after the third month. **1:9. What's the matter.** Terach's suspicion stems from his loyalty to the religion of Nimrod, which has condemned all male babies to death. Terach's idolatry is so complete and profound, he is prepared to carry out the king's decree, even at the cost of his son's life!

D'rash: 1:1. The Maggid said. The inclusion of the Maggid's voice lends authority to the midrash by attesting to the fact that this tale of Abraham is part of a time-honored tradition, presented in the name of a teacher. Thus, we read in *Pirkei Avot* 4:14 in the name of Rabbi N'hora-i: "...And do not rely upon your own understanding." Bartenura interprets this to mean that a teacher's message cannot be fully understood or properly appreciated unless one hears the message directly from the instructor. Since the term *maggid* may commonly refer to a "preacher," its use here also reminds the reader that the story is one of religious significance, an extended hortatory sermon, as it were.

1:13 She said to him, "Every year
this sickness happens to me,
1:15 which is called *kolitzni*."
Terach said to her, "Show me
1:17 your belly, because it seems to me
that you're pregnant, and if so,
1:19 it is not proper to transgress
the commandment of our god,
1:21 Nimrod."

אָמְרָה לוֹ, "בְּכָל שָׁנָה
אֵירַע לִי זֶה חוֹלִי
שֶׁיִּקְרָא אוֹתוֹ קוֹלִצְנִי."
אָמַר לָהּ תֶּרַח, "הַרְאֵינִי
בִּטְנֵךְ שֶׁנִּרְאָה לִי
שְׁאַתְּ מְעוּבֶּרֶת, וְאִם כָּךְ הוּא
אֵין רָאוּי לַעֲבוֹר
אֶת מִצְוַת אֱלֹהֵינוּ
נִמְרוֹד."

P'shat: **1:15. kolitzni.** The term apparently indicates a type of medical condition manifested in a swelling and/or hardening of the belly. **1:16. Terach said.** Terach here again shows that he is a true believer in the religion of Nimrod. **1:20. commandment of our god.** The term "commandment," or *mitzvah* (מִצְוָה) in Hebrew, indicates a religious obligation that necessarily proceeds from the One, true God. The mitzvah system, the program of behaviors designed to make God's will concrete in this world, stands at the very heart of Judaism. **1:20. our god.** King Nimrod ruled over civilization then and had declared himself a god.

D'rash: **1:15. kolitzni.** This obvious loan word is spelled differently in each of the extant printed and manuscript editions of the midrash. It may be related to the Italian, *calcinaccio*, referring to a "hardening of the belly." **1:16. Terach said.** The fact that Abraham, a righteous individual, stems from Terach, an arrant idolater, speaks of Abraham's praiseworthiness. It also indicates to us that whatever our parental background and/or sins of the past, we can still grow to accomplish righteous goals in the world. We can still elevate ourselves to attain the reality of our "higher selves." The High Holy Day experience can be part of this sacred process. **1:20. commandment of our god.** This phrase occurs in Ezra 10:3 in the context of establishing a covenant with the One God to act "according to the council of the Eternal" in the matter of Jewish continuity. Therefore, in its place here, referring to the instructions of Nimrod, it points to the irony of a human being attempting to arrogate himself beyond the healthy limits of human mortality to masquerade as a god. While God's "mitzvot" are good, sanctifying, and spiritually elevating, Nimrod's commandments are murderous, driving adherents to sin. **1:21. Nimrod.** The first extant reference to Nimrod occurs in chapter 10 of the Book of Genesis, as a son of Cush. The text describes him as גִּבּוֹר צַיִד *(gibur tzayid)*, "a mighty hunter" (Genesis 10:9). This echoes the description of Esau found in Genesis 25:27, אִישׁ יֹדֵעַ צַיִד *(ish yodei-a tzayid)*, "a man who knows how to hunt." Since rabbinic tradition regards Esau negatively as a stand-in for "the nations" (that is, the "others" who do not share the values or moral behaviors of the people Israel)—in particular, Rome, the oppressor of the Jewish people, destroyer of the Second Temple and the Jewish religion—so too may Nimrod be regarded in the same light. *B'reishit Rabbah* (37:2) understands the term "hunter" metaphorically when applied to Nimrod. That is, he "ensnared" people with his words and caused them to rebel against God. In fact, the *Zohar* (1:73b) notes that the very name Nimrod stems from the Hebrew root מרד (*m-r-d*), "to rebel." Sforno opines that Nimrod's insistence on one state religion stemmed solely from the agenda of consolidating his rulership. *B'reishit Rabbah* (37:3) includes both Nimrod and Esau on its "top-six list" of evil biblical characters, along with the following enemies of Judaism: Datan and Abiram, who, as allies with Korach, led a rebellion against the leadership of Moses and Aaron in the wilderness and whose essence, according to the Rabbis, was to deny the divine authority of the Torah; King Ahaz, ruler of Judah who made molten images and burnt his own children in the valley of Hinnom as sacrifices to the pagan gods; and King Ahasuerus of Persia (and Purim infamy), who not only endorsed a plot to murder all the Jews, but according to the Talmud, profaned the holy vessels of the First Temple.

1:22	But when he put his hand upon her belly, the Holy One, blessed be He,	וְכַאֲשֶׁר שָׂם יָדוֹ עַל בִּטְנָהּ עָשָׂה לָהּ הַקָּדוֹשׁ בָּרוּךְ הוּא
1:24	performed a miracle for her and the boy rose higher	נֵס גָּדוֹל וְהָלַךְ הַיֶּלֶד לְמַעֲלָה תַּחַת הֶחָזֶה.
1:26	in her chest. He felt with his hands but did not find a thing. He said	וּפִשְׁפֵּשׁ בְּיָדָיו וְלֹא מָצָא שׁוּם דָּבָר. אָמַר
1:28	to her, "You are right in what you said."	לָהּ, "צוֹדֶקֶת בְּמַה שֶּׁאָמַרְתּ."
1:30	So the pregnancy was neither noticeable nor known until the	וְלֹא נִרְאָה הַדָּבָר וְלֹא נוֹדַע עַד
1:32	gestation period was completed. But, due to her great fear,	שֶׁנִּשְׁלְמוּ חָדְשֵׁי הַיֶּלֶד. וּמֵרוֹב פַּחְדָּהּ
1:34	she went forth from the city, and walked in the wilderness near	יָצְאָה מִן הָעִיר וְהָלְכָה דֶּרֶךְ הַמִּדְבָּר קָרוֹב
1:36	a river.	לְנָהָר אֶחָד.

P'shat: **1:24. miracle.** Abraham's survival is not a coincidence. Rather, Abraham's emergence is the purposeful work of the Master of the universe. **1:25. boy rose.** The "boy" in this case is the unborn Abraham. **1:26. in her chest.** God not only moved Abraham higher into his mother's body, but miraculously created enough space there, in her chest, to do so. **1:28. You are right.** Terach believed this to be a case of *kolitzni* (the disease that causes hardening of the belly), as his wife had stated. **1:33. great fear.** If the baby were discovered, he would be murdered in accordance with Nimrod's decree.

D'rash: **1:24. miracle**. *Sh'mot Rabbah* reports a legend concerning the Jewish babies born during the oppression of Egypt. The midrash teaches that when the Egyptians came to look for the infants to kill them, God performed a miracle and the infants were swallowed up by the ground until the Egyptians left. Thus, we read in Exodus 1:7, "The Children of Israel were fruitful and increased abundantly...the *land was filled with them.*" This is one of the many parallels between the story of the Exodus from Egypt and the redemption of Abraham. **1:27. did not find**. This may be thought to parallel Exodus 2:2, "she hid him," alluding to the hiding of the infant Moses by his mother, Yocheved. **1:33. great fear**. Nimrod's decree echoes that of the Pharaoh of the Exodus: "And Pharaoh charged all his people, saying: 'Every son that is born you shall cast into the river...'" (Exodus 1:22). **1:35–36. near a river**. This again reflects the story of the baby Moses, whose mother took him down by a river when she could no longer hide him. As we read in Exodus 2:3, "When she could no longer hide him, she took for him an ark of bulrushes and daubed it with slime and with pitch, and she put the child therein and laid it in the reeds by the river's brink."

1:37 She found a large cave there,	וּמָצְאָה שָׁם מַעֲרָה גְדוֹלָה
and entered it. Then the next day,	וְנִכְנְסָה לְשָׁם. וּלְמָחָר
1:39 birth pangs gripped her,	אֲחָזוּהָ חֶבְלֵי יוֹלֶדֶת
and she gave birth to a son.	וַתֵּלֶד בֵּן.
1:41 And she saw the entire cave	וַתֵּרָאָה אֶת הַמַּעֲרָה כּוּלָה
illuminated as if by the sun from	מְאִירָה כַּשֶּׁמֶשׁ מָאוֹר
1:43 the light of the face of the child.	פְּנֵי הַיֶּלֶד
And she was very happy.	וַתִּשְׂמַח שִׂמְחָה גְדוֹלָה.
1:45 And the child was Abraham our Patriarch,	וְהוּא הָיָה אַבְרָהָם אָבִינוּ,
may peace be upon him.	עָלָיו הַשָּׁלוֹם.
1:47 She cried out and said,	וּפָתְחָה פִּיהָ וְאָמְרָה,
"Woe! For I who have given birth to you	"אוֹי שִׁילַדְתִּיךְ
1:49 at this time when	בַּזְּמַן הַזֶּה
1:50 King Nimrod reigns."	שֶׁמָּלֵךְ נִמְרוֹד".

P'shat: **1:44. very happy**. The shining face of the infant triggers an unexpected moment of spiritual exaltation, despite the dire circumstances of his birth. **1:48. Woe!** Hebrew: אוֹי *(Oy!)*. The mother's joy over the divine miracle of life is interrupted by her sudden recollection of the earthly king's murderous rampage.

D'rash: **1:41–42. cave illuminated**. *Sh'mot Rabbah* and Babylonian Talmud, *Sotah* 12a both report of Moses' birth, "The entire house was flooded with light." These sources derive the illumination through an interpretive technique known as *g'zeirah shavah*. This technique draws homiletic lessons between two or more scriptural texts based upon the appearance of similar phrases found in both texts. In the case of the illumination of Moses' face at birth, we read in both Exodus 2:2, "And when she saw him that *he was good*," and Genesis 1:4, "And God saw the light that *it was good*." This comparison gives rise to the conclusion that both events (and by its parallel nature, the birth of Abraham) mark the creation of a new moral order fraught with the possibilities of sharing the divine light of the spirit. **1:43. light of the face.** This echoes the description of Moses found in Exodus 34:29, "When Moses descended from Mount Sinai, with the two tablets of the Testimony in his hand, he did not know that the skin of his face had become radiant as God had spoken to him." Thus, light serves as a metaphor for holiness and closeness to God. Proverbs 6:23 relates that "the Torah is light." And the *Zohar* describes Abraham, who spread Torah, as the "light" of his family and birthplace.

1:51 "He has killed more than seventy-thousand males because of you.	״וְהָרַג בַּעֲבוּרְךָ מִשִּׁבְעִים אֶלֶף זְכָרִים.
1:53 And I am very afraid for you, for if he knows of you, he will kill you.	וַאֲנִי אֶפְחַד עָלֶיךָ מְאֹד שֶׁאִם יֵדַע בְּךָ יַהֲרֹג.
1:55 So because of this, it is better that you die in this cave	וְעַל זֶה יוֹתֵר טוֹב שֶׁתָּמוּת בַּמְּעָרָה הַזֹּאת
1:57 so that my eyes will not see you slaughtered upon my bosom."	וְלֹא יִרְאוּךָ עֵינַי שָׁחוּט עַל חָזֶה שֶׁלִּי.״
1:59 So she took from the clothing that was upon her	וְלָקְחָה מַלְבּוּשׁ אֲשֶׁר עָלֶיהָ
1:61 and dressed him, and she left him in the cave.	וְהִלְבִּישָׁה אוֹתוֹ וַעֲזָבַתּוּ בַּמְּעָרָה,
1:63 Then she said, "May your God be with you, may He not fail you,	וְאָמְרָה, ״יְהִי אֱלֹהֶיךָ עִמְּךָ לֹא יַרְפְּךָ
1:65 nor forsake you," and she went on her way.	וְלֹא יַעַזְבֶךָ.״ וְהָלְכָה לְדַרְכָּהּ.

P'shat: **1:52. because of you.** The illumination has alerted her to the fact that her son is indeed the one whom Nimrod fears will usurp the king's religion and, hence, the true object of his murderous rampage. **1:63. Then she said.** The seeming hopelessness of the situation pushes Abraham's mother to prayer. **1:63–64. your God.** The utilization of this phrase, as opposed to "our God," indicates that even in the face of the shining, divine miracle of life, Abraham's mother remains an idolater.

D'rash: **1:57. my eyes will not see**. This is similar to the story of Hagar and Ishmael, as related in Genesis 21, the traditional Torah reading for the first day of Rosh HaShanah. Like Abraham's mother, Hagar takes Ishmael to the wilderness. When she finishes all of her water, out of hopelessness she places her baby beneath a shrub. "She went and sat herself down at a distance, some bowshots away, for she said, 'Let me not see the death of the child.'" (Genesis 21:16). Thus, in sending Hagar and Ishmael off to experience the ordeal in the wilderness, the Patriarch is not asking the pair to do anything that he and his mother have not personally experienced. In both cases, God remembers the child, hears his crying, and saves him. This relates to the Rosh HaShanah Shofar Service, one of the themes of which is God's "Remembrance," when we pray that God hear and accept the wail of the ram's horn. **1:64–65. not fail you, nor forsake you**. This echoes Deuteronomy 31:8, which depicts Moses charging Joshua with the responsibility of inheriting the Promised Land: "The Eternal, He is the One who goes before you. He will be with you. He will not fail you, nor forsake you. Fear not and do not be dismayed." We find the identical phrase utilized in I Chronicles 28:20, spoken by King David to his son Solomon regarding the building of the Temple in Jerusalem: "'Be strong and of good courage and do it. Fear not and do not be dismayed, for the Eternal, my God, is with you. He will not fail you, nor forsake you, until all the work for the service of the House of the Eternal will be finished.'" Thus, the prayer of Abraham's mother can be understood as a charge to a holy mission.

1:66	The Maggid said	אָמַר הַמַּגִּיד
	that Abraham our Patriarch,	שֶׁאַבְרָהָם אָבִינוּ,
1:68	may peace be upon him, was still in	עָלָיו הַשָּׁלוֹם, בְּעוֹדוֹ
	the cave; a small boy with no	בַּמְּעָרָה יֶלֶד קָטָן וְלֹא הָיָה
1:70	wet nurse to suckle him. He cried,	מִינֶקֶת שֶׁתְּנִיקֵהוּ. בָּכָה,
	and the Eternal, may He be blessed,	וְשָׁמַע הַשֵּׁם יִתְבָּרַךְ
1:72	heard his crying	בְּכַיָּיתוֹ
	and sent Gabriel the angel to keep	וְשָׁלַח לְגַבְרִיאֵל הַמַּלְאָךְ לְחִיּוֹת
1:74	him alive and give him milk;	אוֹתוֹ וְלָתֵת לוֹ חָלָב,
	in that he brought forth milk from	כִּי הָיָה מוֹצִיא לוֹ חָלָב
1:76	his right forefinger. And he	מֵאֶצְבָּעוֹ הַיָּמִין. וְהָיָה
	suckled from it until he was ten	יוֹנֵק מִמֶּנּוּ עַד שֶׁהָיָה אַבְרָהָם בֶּן עֲשָׂרָה
1:78	days old.	יָמִים.

P'shat: **1:72. heard**. God's "hearing" connotes the quality of divine mercy. **1:76. right forefinger**. The Hebrew may refer to either Gabriel's finger or the baby's. **1:77–78. ten days old**. Abraham miraculously reaches maturity in only ten days.

D'rash: 1:73. Gabriel. As depicted in rabbinic literature, Gabriel is one of the four archangels, members of God's permanent retinue. The archangels represent various aspects of the Godhead, hence, God's unity. The name Gabriel means "God is my strength." In this case, divine might obviously includes "motherly" sustenance. **1:74. give him milk.** This parallels the midrashic tradition that suggests that Mordecai suckled Esther. As we read in *B'reishit Rabbah* 30:8, "R. Y'hudah said, 'On one occasion he went round to all the wet nurses but could not find one for Esther, whereupon he himself suckled her.' R. Berechiah and R. Abbahu in R. Elazar's name said, 'Milk came to him and he suckled her.' " **1:75. milk.** *Sh'mot Rabbah* 23:8 depicts God providing a full range of providence. During the epic of Egyptian slavery, when the Hebrews would go and give birth in the fields to overcome Pharaoh's murderous decrees, R. Yonatan reports that God would descend in Glory, as it were, and cut the umbilical cord, wash and anoint the babies. The Holy One then placed two flints (cakes, according to Babylonian Talmud, *Sotah* 11b) in the baby's hand. One flint flowed with oil, and out of the other came honey and meal. **1:77. suckled.** The *Tz'einah Ur'einah* to Genesis 15:7 applies this legend of the stones to Abraham's sustenance, claiming that one stone flowed with oil, and out of the other came honey and meal. **1:77. from it.** *B'reishit Rabbah* 39:3 interprets this figuratively: "No breasts suckled him in piety and good deeds." That is, Abraham had no one else in his generation from whom to draw religious inspiration, making the Patriarch's spiritual breakthroughs all the more remarkable. At the same time, though, the Sages teach that all of us are born with the capacity for good. It is our mission in life to realize this potential.

GLEANINGS

Trials of Abraham

Abraham, our Patriarch, was tested with ten trials, and he withstood all of them. And the Blessed God revealed before him that in the future his descendants would test the Holy One, blessed be He, ten times. But the cure precedes the sickness, therefore God tested him [Abraham] ten times. The first trial occurred when Abraham, our Patriarch, was born and the high officers of Nimrod sought to kill him, and he hid beneath the earth.

Pirkei D'Rabbi Eliezer, chapter 26

Trials Today

My father used to say, "Show me a person who has no problems and I'll show you a fool." Too many Jews today want to solve everything, find simple solutions and answers—as if all we have are simple questions—when actually we have profound and exciting problems. I like the struggle and the conflicts. I don't want to live in a fool's paradise.

Susannah Heschel, "Contradictions," in *The Invisible Thread*, ed. Diana Bletter and Lori Grinker (Philadelphia: Jewish Publication Society, 1989), page 24

Clothes Make the Man?

R. Y'hudah said: The garment of glory that the Holy One made for Adam and for his wife was with Noah in the ark. When they left the ark, Noah's son Ham took it, brought it out with him, and bequeathed it to Nimrod. Whenever Nimrod wore it, all cattle, beasts, and fowl, upon seeing the garment on him, would come and prostrate themselves before him. Now, human beings supposed that the greatness of Nimrod's own strength brought about such adoration, and so they made him king over them.

Pirkei D'Rabbi Eliezer, chapter 24

The Miracle

So it felt embarrassing, a social liability, to admit an interest in God....But then I gave birth two and a half years ago. That was such a miracle that it's hard not to try to figure out how to address it. The manifest miraculousness of having your child wake up in the morning and look at you! It's hard not to speculate about "where did you come from?" The kind of love that being a parent brings out, that donkey-like, repetitive, abject, egoless love, is closer to a spiritual notion of love than any other kind of love I've experienced....This kind of experience of love made it easier for me to understand some of what the spiritual traditions were addressing.

Naomi Wolf, "Starting on My Spiritual Path," *Tikkun* 13 (January/February 1998): 18

Revelation

When the Israelites came to the Sea, and their children with them, and the latter beheld God at the Sea, they said to their parents: "This is the One who did all those things for us when we were in Egypt," as it says, "This is my God, and I will glorify Him." [Exodus 15:2].

Sh'mot Rabbah 23:8

Torah the Milk

There has always been a dialectic tension in Judaism between transcendence and immanence. In Rabbinic Judaism the pendulum swung well over to the side of transcendence; feminist Judaism is pulling the pendulum back. We need to explore these different images of God in our tradition—the image in the midrash of God as a nursing mother with Torah the milk she gives her child Israel, the image of the Shechinah, the God who is the source of *Rachamim,* womb-like compassion, the God Jacob/Israel saw in the face of his brother.

Laura Geller, "Symposium: What Kind of Tikkun Does the World Need?" *Tikkun* 1 (fall 1986): 110

A Prayer

With all my heart, with all my soul, with all my might,
I pray for the health of this child.
I pray for it to be perfect in mind and body,
To issue safely and easily from me
At the proper time,
To grow steadily and sturdily
In a home filled with joy at its presence,
To be nurtured into a person who greets the world
with passion, enthusiasm, dance, love, humility, faith.

Judy Shanks, quoted in *The New Jewish Baby Book,* by Anita Diamant (Woodstock, Vt.: Jewish Lights, 1993), page 7

Light

Was the light really created on the first day? It is written: "God set them [the sun, moon, and stars] in the firmament of heaven" [Genesis 1:17], about which it says, "There was evening and there was morning, a *fourth day*" [Genesis 1:19]....Rabbi Elazar said: In the light that the Holy One created on the first day, one could see from one end of the world to the other; but as soon as the Holy One beheld the generation of the Flood and the generation of the Tower of Babel, and saw that their actions were corrupt, God arose and hid it from them, for it is said, "Light is withheld from the wicked" [Job 38:15]. Then for whom did God reserve it? For the righteous in the time to come, for it is said, "God saw that the light was *good*" [Genesis 1:4]. "Good" is an allusion not to the light but to the righteous for whom it is reserved, as it is said, "Say of the righteous that they are good" [Isaiah 3:10].

Babylonian Talmud, *Chagigah* 12a

Light Is Hope

What happened is not what God intended. Even in the camp I tried to be positive. One time we were supposed to go to the gas chambers but there was no room for us. I always imagined that in the next hour something might happen to make things better. Even as a little girl I was taught that I shouldn't give up...that tomorrow might bring a change.

Judaism is a very positive religion. Jews have suffered throughout history but we've always had some kind of light to hold onto. We are the people of hope.

Tova Berger, in *The Invisible Thread,* ed. Diana Bletter and Lori Grinker (Philadelphia: Jewish Publication Society, 1989), page 75

Torah Is Light

R. Abbahu returned from a journey with his face illuminated. A student inquired, "Have you discovered a treasure?" "Yes," replied the Rabbi, "I have discovered an ancient *Tosefta* [passage of the Oral Torah]."

Babylonian Talmud, *N'darim* 49a

The Ten Trials of Abraham

As noted above, tradition has it that en route to achieving his divinely ordained destiny and becoming the person God meant him to be, Abraham undergoes ten trials. Although the number ten is generally agreed upon, it should surprise no one familiar with the history of Jewish thought to know that there is disagreement as to which episodes in the life of the Patriarch should be included among the count. Maimonides enumerates only those trials mentioned from Genesis, chapters 12 through 22 (from the command לֶךְ לְךָ *[lech l'cha],* "go forth" from your country, to לֶךְ לְךָ *[lech l'cha],* "go forth" to the land of Moriah and raise your son up there as an offering—the *Akeidah* or Binding of Isaac). *Pirkei D'Rabbi Eliezer* and *Avot D'Rabbi Natan* list trials from the midrashic tradition as well, including two of the episodes represented in *Maaseh Avraham Avinu.*

Pirkei D'Rabbi Eliezer identifies Abraham's ten trials as follows: (1) Nimrod seeks to kill Abraham and the latter hides in a cave; (2) Nimrod throws Abraham into the fiery furnace of Ur of the Chaldees; (3) Abraham leaves his country; (4) famine in the land of Canaan; (5) Sarah is taken to Pharaoh's palace; (6) Abraham's battle with the four kings in order to rescue his nephew Lot; (7) the "Covenant between the Pieces" in which God informs Abraham of the future exile of his descendants; (8) the commandment to circumcise himself and his son Ishmael; (9) the commandment to expel Ishmael and his mother, Hagar; (10) the *Akeidah.*

Pirkei Avot (5:3) reports that "Abraham was tested ten times and withstood them all." But the text does not identify any of the trials individually. *Pirkei Avot* does, however, place the ten tests within a context of "tens." Thus, the first mishnah of chapter 5 begins by teaching that God created the world with ten statements. The next mishnah teaches that there were ten generations from Adam to Noah, when God brought the Flood, and then another ten generations from Noah to Abraham. The third mishnah of chapter 5 then reports the ten trials of Abraham, with the following mishnah (number four of chapter 5) attesting to the ten miracles performed for our ancestors in Egypt and ten at the Sea.

Within this context, it is possible to discern the correspondence of the ten statements with which God created the world with the two sets of ten generations that follow, for each set of ten generations eventually brings a "re-creation" of the world—once at the time of the Flood, with Noah as the vehicle of renewal, and again with the emergence of Abraham, who helps re-create the world in a moral-ethical sense. *B'reishit Rabbah* 12:9 points out that when we read, in Genesis 2:4, "These are the generations of the heavens and the earth when He [God] created them" (בְּהִבָּרְאָם, *b'hibaram*), the letters can be rearranged to spell בְּאַבְרָהָם (*b'Avraham*), "with Abraham." That is, God created the world "with Abraham."

Looking forward, *Pirkei D'Rabbi Natan* argues for a cause-and-effect relationship between Abraham's ten trials and the miracles performed for our ancestors in Egypt and at the Sea as well. So we see that Abraham's meeting the challenges of the trials that have come his way not only illustrates his greatness and his prodigious love for God, but serves as a bedrock for Judaism, paving the way for the Exodus from Egypt.

Like Abraham, we too experience trials in our lives. We have all been tested, in one way or another. Our challenge is to place these trials in perspective, so that we may use them as stepping-stones to personal growth. This viewing and reviewing of the trials of our lives, this *cheshbon hanefesh*, or "accounting of the soul," is an integral part of the High Holy Day process. But even more critical than gaining perspective are the actions that emerge from our trials. Abraham showed his love for God by responding to his tests with deeds of loving-kindness, and this avenue is open to us as well. Acting with righteousness lends meaning to our struggles, purpose to our lives, and healing to the world. Every act of kindness counts. Our text teaches that Abraham's righteous behavior throughout the ten trials gave birth to twenty miracles. In much the same way, *Pirkei Avot* teaches: The reward for a mitzvah is a mitzvah.

Mitzvot

The Hebrew term *mitzvah* (מִצְוָה), which is often understood to connote a good deed, literally means "commandment," a sacred obligation. Performing a mitzvah is doing what God wants. For Jews, the commandments constitute the path to moral living and holiness.

Jewish tradition maintains that the Torah reveals 613 commandments. In Hebrew, these are commonly known as the תרי"ג מִצְוֹת, or *Taryag Mitzvot*. (The phrase reflects the fact that the Rabbis assign each Hebrew letter a numerical equivalent. The ת equals 400, ר = 200, י = 10, and the ג = 3.) Although the total of 613 commandments is generally agreed upon, there exists disagreement as to exactly what they are. Various scholars over the centuries have drawn up their own lists.

The Talmud (*Makot* 23b) teaches that there are 248 positive mitzvot (מִצְוֹת עֲשֵׂה [*mitzvot aseih]*, commandments to do something), thought to correspond to the organs of the body (and also corresponding to the numerical equivalent of Abraham's Hebrew name, אַבְרָהָם; א=1, ב=2, ר=200, ה=5, מ=40 = 248); and 365 negative commandments (מִצְוֹת לֹא תַעֲשֶׂה [*mitzvot lo taaseh]*, commandments to refrain from doing something), one for each day of the solar year. The message, therefore, is one of completeness and commitment. That is, strive to do God's will all the time with a whole heart.

The Rabbis have also offered various other classifications of the mitzvot. A commandment may be either "severe" or "light." These designations, however, have only to do with the penalty prescribed for nonobservance and not the ultimate importance of the particular precept in question. As such, *Pirkei Avot* (2:1) reports: "Rabbi Y'hudah HaNasi was fond of saying, 'Be as careful in the performance of a light mitzvah as [what seems to be] a severe commandment, since you do not know the reward for [the performance of any of] the commandments.'"

Some mitzvot obviously concern our direct relationship with God. The precepts surrounding worship and respect for God's name serve as examples. These types of injunctions are known as מִצְוֹת בֵּין אָדָם לַמָּקוֹם *(mitzvot bein adam lamakom)*, commandments between human beings and God. Other precepts seek to regulate our dealings with other people. The Rabbis refer to these as מִצְוֹת בֵּין אָדָם לַחֲבֵרוֹ *(mitzvot bein adam l'chaveiro)*, commandments between a person and his fellow. But even this latter category comes beneath the aegis of divine concern, for Judaism considers God a partner in each business deal and every marriage. On the High Holy Days, when doing penance for a sin in the category "between a person and his fellow," one must first make restitution and peace with the wronged party. But then one must turn to God for forgiveness as well.

Finally, Maimonides claims that if one possessed the capacity of sufficient insight and were to study hard enough, one would be able to perceive the reasons behind all the commandments. As yet, however, the reasoning underlying some of the mitzvot remains obscure. In reference to the commandments, the Torah speaks of "judgments" (מִשְׁפָּטִים, *mishpatim*) and "ordinances" (חֻקִּים, *chukim*). To the rabbinic mind "judgments" refers to the precepts of civil and criminal law. These commandments are, for the most part, logical and ethical. That we should not murder, for instance, makes perfect sense, for society could not exist without such a "judgment." On the other hand, the Rabbis see the "ordinances" of the Torah as those mitzvot for which we as human beings cannot find logical reasons. Commandments concerning purity of diet (the only type of land animals that the Torah deems pure are those that have completely cloven hooves and chew their cud) and the precepts of the red heifer (the ashes of which, when correctly applied, possess the power to cleanse one from the impurity of contact with the dead while rendering those who prepare these ashes impure) serve as examples of ordinances. Rabbi Lawrence Kushner maintains that these incomprehensible commandments have value in that they constitute a gift of self, performed out of love. Hence, their performance helps us draw closer to God in relationship.

Rabbi Eugene Borowitz puts it this way: "Being Jews, we know that to be human is to be responsible for our actions in some cosmically important way. We may find it easiest to talk of living by our values, but when we must explain why our people chooses to emphasize just the ones it does, we must acknowledge that even we live out of a sense of being commanded" (*Reform Judaism Today*, book 3 [New York: Behrman House, 1983], page 121).

Chapter 2

God's Unity: Abraham Discovers God

Although Abraham's survival and physical maturity (in only ten days!) have been assured through divine intervention, theologically he remains immature. On the positive side, the cave not only guarded his life physically, but protected Abraham from the negative influences of the idolatrous world around him. Thus, Abraham emerges as a blank slate.

The Talmud teaches that all is in the hands of heaven, save for the "awe of heaven." It is our own task to discover God for ourselves. Even God can lead us only so far. Ultimately, our perception of God in the world and the divine potentiality within ourselves depend upon our own efforts and open-mindedness. Abraham's divine discoveries and ongoing relationship with the Creator serve as a model for us, his spiritual progeny.

People often assert that they don't attend synagogue, study Torah, or, in general, live a Jewish lifestyle because they're not sure they believe in God. But there is value in doing these things in any case, for by showing up and participating with the community, they may indeed "find" God. That is, God responds to our yearnings and efforts for divine encounter in our lives when we least expect it, just as God responds to Abraham in the midrash.

This chapter begins with the theological challenge and the very human need to find God. Abraham proves himself equal to this task, combining his experience of the world with a healthy dose of trial-and-error logic.

2:1	And he began to walk about	וְהִתְחִיל לָלֶכֶת
	and went out of the cave and walked	בָּאָרֶץ מֵהַמְּעָרָה וַיֵּלֶךְ
2:3	along the river's edge.	עַל שְׂפַת הַנָּהָר.
	When the sun set and the stars came out,	וּכְשֶׁבָּא (כְּשֶׁשָּׁקַע) הַשֶּׁמֶשׁ וְיָצְאוּ
2:5	he said, "These are the gods."	הַכּוֹכָבִים, הוּא אָמַר, "אֵלּוּ הֵם הָאֱלֹהִים".
	Afterward, when dawn broke,	אַחַר כָּךְ כְּשֶׁעָלָה עַמּוּד הַשַּׁחַר
2:7	he did not see the stars.	לֹא רָאָה הַכּוֹכָבִים,
	He said, "I will not serve these [stars]	אָמַר, "לֹא אֶעֱבוֹד אֶת אֵלּוּ
2:9	because they are not gods."	כִּי אֵינָם אֱלֹהִים".

15

P'shat: **2:2. walked**. Abraham's feat of walking at only ten days of chronological age is indicative of God having miraculously brought him to maturity. **2:5. These are the gods**. The fact that Abraham's first actions upon emerging from the protective ''womb'' of the cave concern identifying God points to the reality of religion as a basic human need. **2:9. are not gods**. Worship of the stars was a common idolatrous tradition in the ancient world. Here, Abraham's speedy rejection of such ideas illustrates their folly.

D'rash: **2:2. out of the cave**. Although the story of Abraham being born, growing up, and/or hiding in a cave appears in many rabbinic sources, the various accounts differ concerning the age of Abraham upon his emergence. While *Maaseh Avraham Avinu* purports the Patriarch to have been ten days old, *Midrash HaGadol* places his age at three years, the age of weaning. *Sefer HaYashar* reports that Abraham left the cave after ten years. This would indicate that he had just attained the age one begins the study of Mishnah, according to R. Y'hudah ben Teima in *Pirkei Avot* 5:21. *Pirkei D'Rabbi Eliezer* depicts Abraham at thirteen years upon his emergence, the age of bar mitzvah and thus the advent of religious responsibility. **2:5. These are the gods**. So prevalent was star worship in ancient days that one of the standard terms throughout rabbinic literature for an idolater is עוֹבֵד כּוֹכָבִים (*oveid kochavim*), ''one who worships [or serves] stars.''

2:10	Afterward, he saw the sun.	אַחַר כָּךְ רָאָה הַשֶּׁמֶשׁ.
	He said, "This is my god,	אָמַר, "זֶה אֵלִי
2:12	and I will glorify it."	וְאַנְוֵהוּ."
	But when the sun set he said,	וּכְשֶׁבָּא הַשֶּׁמֶשׁ אָמַר,
2:14	"This is not God."	"אֵין זֶה אֱלוֹהַּ."
	He saw the moon. He said,	רָאָה הַיָּרֵחַ אָמַר,
2:16	"This is my god, and I will glorify	"זֶה אֵלִי וְאַנְוֵהוּ
	and serve it."	וְאֶעֱבוֹד אוֹתוֹ."
2:18	But when it became dark he said,	כְּשֶׁהֶחְשִׁיךְ אָמַר,
	"This is not God. They have	"אֵין זֶה אֱלוֹהַּ, יֵשׁ לָהֶם
2:20	a force that moves them."	מֵנִיעַ."

P'shat: **2:10. the sun**. Sun worship again serves an example of idolatrous behavior. **2:18. when it became dark**. That is, the moon was no longer visible. Some texts of *Maaseh Avraham Avinu*, however, leave out reference to the moon. Therefore, the ''becoming dark'' once again points to the setting of the sun. **2:20. a force that moves them**. Abraham comes to understand that God is above nature. That is, God creates and controls nature, and not the other way around.

D'rash: **2:10. the sun**. Sun worship was a well-attested practice in ancient Egypt, where the Children of Israel resided in slavery for hundreds of years. Hence, the declaration made by the participants in the water-drawing ceremony of the Festival of Sukkot is described in the Mishnah: "Our ancestors, when they were in this place, they turned with their backs unto the Temple and their faces toward the East, and they worshiped the sun eastward" (*Mishnah Sukkah*). (This statement, in turn, reflects that of Ezekiel 8:16 concerning the sins of the Israelites.) **2:11. This is my god**. This statement alludes to Exodus 15:2, the Song of the Sea "This is my God, and I will glorify Him"), in which Moses and the Children of Israel praise the One God for His mastery over nature and incursion into human history, as witnessed at the Sea of Reeds during the Exodus from Egypt. **2:20. a force**. Parallel accounts of Abraham's discovery of God exist. Again, the various sources depict this occurrence to take place at different stages in the life of the Patriarch. Thus, it can be understood that the discovery of God does not rely upon chronology. Spirituality is not the province of any one age. **2:20. a force that moves them**. One popular name for God in philosophical circles is the "Prime Mover." That is, God is the Creator who originally set the universe in motion. According to the philosophers, God's reality can be discerned through logic, the method that Abraham so successfully employs.

2:21 While he was still speaking,	עוֹדֶנּוּ מְדַבֵּר
Gabriel the angel came	וְהִנֵּה בָּא הַמַּלְאָךְ גַּבְרִיאֵל
2:23 and said to him,	וַאֲמֶר לוֹ,
"Peace unto you, Abraham."	"שָׁלוֹם עָלֶיךָ, אַבְרָהָם."

P'shat: **2:22. Gabriel the angel**. The Hebrew word for angel, מַלְאָךְ (*malach*), actually means "messenger." In this case, God has sent His emissary to Abraham in response to the latter's longing to have God in his life. **2:24. Peace unto you**. This phrase, שָׁלוֹם עָלֶיךָ (*shalom alecha*; pl., שָׁלוֹם עֲלֵיכֶם, *shalom aleichem*) is a typical Hebrew greeting.

D'rash: **2:22. Gabriel the angel**. Although various midrashic traditions depicting Abraham's discovery of God exist, they all bear the common feature of God responding to Abraham's striving. We have the power to move God. If we reach out to God, the Holy One will be sensitive to our strivings and be there for us. Coming to synagogue on the High Holy Days and searching for God is not a useless activity. Jewish tradition assures us that if we search, we will indeed find God. **2:24. Peace**. *B'midbar Rabbah* teaches: so great is the issue and blessing of peace that the prophets decreed it be used as a greeting, one Jew to the next. **2:24. Peace unto you**. *Pirkei D'Rabbi Eliezer* attests to Abraham's speaking the Holy Tongue (Hebrew) upon emergence from the cave. This points to the special place of Hebrew as the language of prayer and Scripture, right from the very birth of our people.

2:25 He said to him,

"Unto you, peace."

אָמַר לוֹ,

"עָלֶיךָ שָׁלוֹם."

2:27 "Who are you?"

He said to him, "I am

אָמַר לוֹ, "מִי אַתָּה?"

אָמַר לוֹ, "אֲנִי

2:29 Gabriel, the angel, an emissary

from the Holy One, blessed

גַּבְרִיאֵל הַמַּלְאָךְ, שָׁלִיחַ

מִן הַקָּדוֹשׁ בָּרוּךְ

2:31 be He."

At that moment he went

הוּא."

בְּעֵת הַהִיא הָלַךְ

2:33 to a spring that he came upon

there, and washed his face,

לְמַעְיָן אֶחָד שֶׁמָּצָא

שָׁם, וְרָחַץ פָּנָיו,

2:35 hands, and feet. Then there he worshiped

God, may He be blessed,

יָדָיו, וְרַגְלָיו. וְהִתְפַּלֵּל

שָׁם לְאֵל יִתְבָּרַךְ

2:37 by bowing down and

prostrating [himself].

בִּכְרִיעָה וְהִשְׁתַּחֲוָיָה.

P'shat: 2:33. spring. Water symbolizes purity and rebirth. **2:34. washed**. Ablutions before prayer are consistent with the system of Jewish law, especially the ancient priestly ritual. **2:37–38. bowing down and prostrating**. Bowing down and prostrating are synonymous with worship.

D'rash: 2:26. Unto you, peace. R. David Luria in his commentary to *Pirkei D'Rabbi Eliezer*, chapter 26, notes that the hour of Abraham's emergence from the cave preceded the dispersion that resulted from Nimrod's Tower of Babel. At this time everyone spoke the Holy Tongue, the language of Creation. As a consequence of their having participated in the sin of the Tower, God confounded the builders' language and dispersed them across the earth. Since Abraham did not participate with Nimrod in the construction of the Tower, only he (and his descendants) remained as speakers of Hebrew. This story, again, points to the importance the Rabbis attached to the Hebrew language as a vehicle for Jewish unity and spirituality. **2:33. spring**. Water, in rabbinic literature, indicates God's life-giving beneficence in both the physical realm and the spiritual sphere. Water, especially in the form of an ever-flowing stream, is a metaphor for Torah. **2:34. washed**. These ablutions prior to prayer echo the priestly Yom Kippur service of ancient days as described in *Mishnah Yoma* (3:3): "No person may enter the Court [of the Temple], even if he were ritually clean, until he had immersed himself. On this day [Yom Kippur] the High Priest immersed five times and sanctified himself ten times." **2:38. prostrating**. Prostration was also a part of the ancient Yom Kippur service, as described in chapters 5 and 6 of *Mishnah Yoma*. In fact, the High Holy Days represent the only times that some Jews still maintain the tradition of prostration. **2:38. prostrating**. The text of the *Aleinu* prayer (found in the Shofar Service of

Rosh HaShanah, as well as at the conclusion of each daily service) parallels the midrash in that, after recognizing God as Creator, it continues, "We bow down and prostrate ourselves, and acknowledge before the supreme Sovereign of sovereigns, the Holy One, blessed be He." **2:38. prostrating**. The Talmud associates Abraham with the origins of prayer by crediting him with creating the Morning Service (שַׁחֲרִית, *Shacharit*). This is derived from Genesis 19:27, "Abraham arose in the morning to the place where he had *stood* before God." For "standing" (עֲמִידָה, *amidah*) connotes praying, as it is written in Psalm 106:30, "Then Pinchas *stood up* and prayed."

GLEANINGS

Lasting Attachment

Were we consciously to face up to our relationship to God and live by it, the uniqueness of our way of life would become far more manifest. Yet even in our current state of relative disbelief and faithlessness, I am suggesting that the source from which the special quality of our people's life comes is its lasting attachment to God.

Eugene Borowitz, *Reform Judaism Today*, book 3 (New York: Behrman House, 1983), page 121

A Parable of Observation

A wanderer was passing a castle. Attempting to find out what was inside, he walked all around to find the entrance, all to no avail. He called loudly, but no one answered. "Could it be that this castle is deserted?" he reflected. He raised his eyes to the roof and found that it had been covered with a protective layer of material, with a second layer carefully arranged above it. "This castle must be inhabited" said the wanderer, "or else who could have arranged the layers on the roof so meticulously?"

Midrash HaGadol 12:1

A World on Fire

Rabbi Yitzchak said: "A man was traveling from place to place when he saw a building in flames. 'Is it possible that the building lacks a person to look after it?' he wondered. The owner of the building looked out and said, 'I am the owner of the building.' Similarly, because Abraham our Patriarch said, 'Is it conceivable that the world is without a guide?' The Holy One, blessed be He, looked out and said to him, 'I am the Guide, the Sovereign of the universe.'"

B'reishit Rabbah 39:1

Age of Hearkening

R. Chanina and R. Yochanan both said: "Abraham was 48 years old when he recognized his Creator." R. Levi said in the name of Reish Lakish: "He was 3 years old, for Abraham hearkened to the voice of his Creator [for as many years as] the numerical value of *eikev* [עֵקֶב]; as we read, 'Because [עֵקֶב] Abraham hearkened to my voice' [Genesis 26:5]." [Since the *g'matria* of the word עֵקֶב is 172 (ע = 70, ק = 100, ב = 2), and the Patriarch's life span was 175 years, one may deduce that Abraham discovered and began hearkening to God's voice at the age of 3.]

B'reishit Rabbah 64:4

The Two Lights

Zaddikim are like the lights up in Heaven. When God created the two great lights of Heaven He placed both in the firmament, each to do its own special service. Ever since, they have been friends. The great light does not boast of being great and the small light is content with being small. And so it was in the days of our sages: there was a whole skyful of stars, large stars and small stars, and they lived together in all brotherliness.

R. Mendel of Rymanov, in *Tales of the Hasidim, Book Two: The Later Masters,* by Martin Buber (New York: Schocken Books, 1947), page 130

Hebrew Language

Hebrew is the primary language of the Jewish people. It was the language of the Bible and of rabbis throughout history. The medieval commentator Rashi, who lived outside of Paris, spoke French, but he wrote his biblical commentary in Hebrew. Maimonides must have spoken to his Egyptian neighbors in Arabic, but he composed his monumental fourteen-book code of Jewish law in Hebrew. So Hebrew is the language of the Jewish spirit.

Morris N. Kertzner, *What Is a Jew?,* revised by Lawrence A. Hoffman (New York: Collier Books, 1953), pages 96–97

Yom Kippur Prostration

When the priests and the people who stood in the Temple court heard the High priest, full of reverence, utter God's holy and awesome Name, they fell upon their faces and, prostrate, exclaimed: "Blessed is God's glorious majesty for ever and ever!"

Afternoon Service for Yom Kippur, *Gates of Repentance,* (New York: CCAR, 1978), page 424

Mikva Dreams

In all the glory of continuing love, the Mikva is a taste of Heaven. She tumbles down into the water, like a fetus, and is reborn to life. Old surfaces gone, non-life gone. Life is holy, to be understood as holy and separated from Death, from dead parts. She is always holy—but she causes a separation to be made between life and non-life.

Mirele Laderman Ukeles, "Mikva Dreams: A Performance," in *Four Centuries of Jewish Women's Spirituality,* ed. Ellen M. Umansky and Dianne Ashton (Boston: Beacon Press, 1992), page 219

What to Pray For

And in those moments when I felt absolutely powerless, something particularly difficult for a person as independent as I am, I prayed for patience and the ability to endure a little more. And when I was too weak to pray, I hoped that God's love would envelop me, that God's embrace would bring me comfort and lift me up from the depths of despair.

Sally J. Priesand, "I Prayed for Wisdom, Courage, Patience," in *The Jewish Woman's Book of Wisdom,* ed. Ellen Jaffe-Gill (Secaucus, N.J.: Birch Lane Press, 1998), page 111

Immersion in Jewish Law and Custom

The practice of immersion in "living waters" (מַיִם חַיִּים, *mayim chayim*) is well attested to in Jewish law and custom. Jewish tradition prescribes immersion for several cases, among them a woman at the end of her menstrual cycle, the Nazirite upon the conclusion of the vow of abstinence, one who experiences a genital emission, a woman who gives birth, a person who has contact with a corpse, a person recovering from skin disease, a convert, an individual who approaches the altar or even enters the Sanctuary, and a bride or groom prior to the wedding.

On one level, immersion may be thought of as a purification against ritual contamination, the main object being to prevent the desecration of the Sanctuary. In his book *Ritual and Morality,* Hyam Maccoby points out that according to biblical law, non-Jews surprisingly do not contract ritual impurity. The whole system of purity as found in the Torah and elaborated upon in rabbinic literature has to do with the concept of Jews as a priestly nation. Thus, immersion becomes part of the "protocol for a dedicated group living constantly in the presence of God, whose Tabernacle is in their midst."

Anita Diamant, in *The New Jewish Wedding,* argues that immersion is not necessarily about "uncleanliness," but about "human encounters with the holy." She points out that the non-Jew who converts to Judaism is required to immerse. The essential issue here is not contamination, but change of status. The convert, through the womb-like "living waters," becomes, in effect, reborn. Upon emerging, the convert is considered a new person. Old family ties may no longer be legally applied. The convert is considered the spiritual progeny of Abraham and Sarah, with a new name, identity, and mission in life.

In much the same way, Abraham's immersion in the midrash represents a change of status. His immersion may be seen as more than just a preparation for worship. Rather, he is passing from his "godless" state to one in which he is actively involved in service to the Holy One. He becomes, in effect, reborn, changed, a new person with a new identity. He is the first convert, the first Jew.

Abraham's immersion serves as a metaphor for our prayers and *t'shuvah* and righteousness during the High Holy Days in that both Abraham's ablutions and our High Holy Day activities bear the promise of catharsis and transformation. The High Holy Day process changes us. Our efforts at prayer, *t'shuvah,* and deeds of kindness allow us to emerge as new, better people. Our rituals and our deeds have the power to lift our status from that of "one who has missed the mark" to that of "purity and holiness," enabling us to begin the year with a new and tender heart.

Water is also a symbol of Torah. Immersion in Torah, defined broadly as the comprehensive enterprise of Jewish study, engenders spiritual rebirth. As the Talmud teaches (*Kiddushin* 40b), learning Torah is of such paramount importance because the study of Torah leads to holy action.

Finally, it should be mentioned that some men and women maintain the custom of immersing themselves in preparation for Yom Kippur. Their immersion may be seen as part of the High Holy Day process of self-improvement, a catharsis from the mistakes of the past. By immersing themselves, they are seeking the opportunity to emerge as new and better people in the year ahead.

Chapter 3

God's Might versus Earthly (Tyrannical) Power: Abraham and Nimrod—The Initial Confrontation

Following Abraham's ablutions and worship, his mother "remembers him" and returns to the scene of his abandonment to find out what has become of him. Walking along the riverbank, Abraham's mother bumps into him and is amazed that a person who is only twenty days old can walk upright, speak, and proclaim the oneness of God. Abraham instructs his mother to go to Nimrod and inform him of God's existence.

Instead, Abraham's mother returns to her husband, Terach, who has become a courtier and official of Nimrod. Terach runs to Nimrod, prostrates himself before his god-king, and apologetically reports the existence of his son, of whose birth he has only just learned. Upon hearing this news, Nimrod trembles. Incapacitated by fear, he requests the advice of his ministers. When they prove less than helpful, Satan (disguised as a man dressed in black silk) enters, prostrates himself before Nimrod, and suggests that the king open the royal arsenals and unleash the full force of royal armed forces against Abraham, with the intention being to capture him and have him serve the king.

Nimrod dispatches the army. In a scene reminiscent of the Israelites looking up to see Pharaoh's chariots charging against them (Exodus 14:10), Abraham sees Nimrod's army rushing toward him. Abraham prays to God. As in the story of the Exodus from Egypt, God places a cloud between the army and Abraham. God then sends Gabriel to miraculously transport Abraham upon his shoulder, in a flash, to Babylonia, the city in which Nimrod resides.

Abraham enters the city and proclaims the unity of God. While proclaiming witness to his Creator in the marketplace, Abraham meets his parents. Back at the family home, Abraham relates his miraculous escape from Nimrod's armed forces. Terach immediately runs to Nimrod to inform him of Abraham's amazing arrival upon the shoulders of God's angel. Nimrod, upon hearing of the wondrous actions of the One God, again trembles. He then follows the advice of his counselors and decrees a seven-day festival during which the great wealth of the nation will be on display. Nimrod hopes to corrupt Abraham and win him over with a fantastic display of gold and silver and embroidery. Predictably unmoved by this show of materialism, Abraham goes to the palace to confront Nimrod directly.

This face-to-face confrontation not only illustrates God's might versus earthly (tyrannical) power played out on the grand scale, but is also suggestive for us of what it means to be God's servant in our own day and age. Nimrod represents the secular authorities and influences of our society, which place great emphasis upon the material, but not the spiritual. Abraham, as a Jew, stands for the spiritual seeker. Sometimes we must be like Abraham and stand up to secular authority and influence. This may mean engaging in social action, lobbying the representatives of government, and fighting on behalf of the great moral issues of our day. A formative childhood memory is that of my rabbi going "down South" to march with Martin Luther King on behalf of the struggle for civil rights. Standing up to secular authority may mean taking off from work, school, or sports practice for the sake of religious observance or principle. At times this may require direct confrontation. This may take the form of a street demonstration, speaking truth to those in power in the public forum of community meetings and/or the media, or even going to court to fight for justice in this world. Other times the conflict may be played out in terms of the allocation of our resources. While the demands made of us may seem limitless, we possess only so much time, energy, and money. Synagogue membership, religious education, support for righteous causes, acts of loving-kindness, and even choosing to keep kosher all tax our resources, causing us to make complicated decisions about how to best use our limited resources.

The chapter begins for Abraham with the challenge of confronting Nimrod, who has actively sought the Patriarch's death, with the truth of God in the world. Through courage, devotion to God, and ever-present humility, Abraham prevails, not only to emerge from the meeting unscathed, but to provide the king and his court, as well as Terach, his father, a vision of God's might. The Patriarch, again, serves as a model for us, his spiritual descendants, by standing up for his beliefs.

3:1	Afterward, as the king, Nimrod, sat upon the throne of his	וַיְהִי אַחֲרֵי כֵן כְּשֶׁבֶת הַמֶּלֶךְ נִמְרוֹד עַל כִּסֵּא
3:3	kingdom, he sent for Abraham to come to him, with his father,	מַלְכוּתוֹ שָׁלַח אַחֲרֵי אַבְרָהָם וַיָּבֹא אֵלָיו וְאָבִיו
3:5	Terach. And Abraham passed before the governors and	תֶרַח עִמּוֹ. וַיַּעֲבֹר אַבְרָהָם לִפְנֵי הַפַּחוֹת
3:7	the officers until he reached the royal throne upon which he was sitting.	וְהַסְּגָנִים עַד שֶׁהִגִּיעַ לְכִסֵּא הַמֶּלֶךְ אֲשֶׁר הוּא יוֹשֵׁב עָלָיו.
3:9	He grasped the throne and shook it and Abraham, our Patriarch, cried out,	וַיִּתְפֹּס בַּכִּסֵּא וְהֶנִיעַ אוֹתוֹ וַיִּקְרָא אַבְרָהָם אָבִינוּ
3:11	in a great voice, words like these: "Alas, Nimrod, the loathsome,	בְּקוֹל גָּדוֹל כִּדְבָרִים הָאֵלֶּה: "אִי נִמְרוֹד הַנִּגְעָל,

23

3:13	the blasphemer, the denier of the	הַכּוֹפֵר בְּעִיקָר,
	living and enduring God and of	וְכוֹפֵר בְּאֵל חַי וְקַיָּם
3:15	Abraham,	וּבְאַבְרָהָם,

P'shat: **3:2. throne**. The throne is a symbol of royal power. **3:5–6. Abraham passed before.** The Patriarch does not bow down before the king, as do other visitors to the palace.

D'rash: **3:2. throne**. Exodus 12:29 describes the plague of the killing of the firstborn as beginning with "the firstborn of Pharaoh, who sits upon his throne." The phrase therefore intimates that royal power is no match for divine strength. **3:2–3. sat upon the throne of his kingdom**. We find the identical phrase in Esther 5:1, introducing the scene where Esther comes before the king as an agent of God to save the Jewish people. Sometimes what it means to be God's servant involves speaking truth to those in power. Doing the right thing can mean displaying the courage to risk loss. **3:6–7. the governors and the officers**. Jeremiah (51:23) uses this term as a metaphor for the sinners of Babylonia who will be shattered by God.

3:16	the faithful servant of His house.	עַבְדוֹ נֶאֱמָן בֵּיתוֹ.
	Attest and declare like me that	תָּעֵיד וְתֹאמַר כָּמוֹנִי
3:18	the Eternal, He is (the One) God,	שֶׁיְיָ הוּא הָאֱלֹהִים אֶחָד
	there is none other. And He has	וְאֵין שֵׁנִי. וְאֵינוֹ
3:20	no corporeality. And He lives	גוּף. וְהוּא חַי
	and will not die. He will neither	וְלֹא יָמוּת וְלֹא
3:22	slumber nor sleep. And you shall	יָנוּם וְלֹא יִישָׁן. וְתָעֵיד
	admit that you are a mortal, and	עַל עַצְמְךָ שֶׁאַתָּה אָדָם
3:24	you shall believe that I,	וְתַאֲמִין שֶׁאֲנִי
	Abraham, am His servant. And	אַבְרָהָם [עַבְדוֹ].
3:26	He created the entire world in	וְהוּא בָּרָא אֶת כָּל הָעוֹלָם
	order that they would believe in	כְּדֵי שֶׁיַאֲמִינוּ."
3:28	Him."	

P'shat: **3:23. admit that you are a mortal**. That is, not a god. The proof is that Nimrod does not possess any of the superhuman qualities here ascribed to God (no corporeality or eternality, rather constant conscious vigilance). **3:26. He created**. God is the Creator, not Nimrod. Again, God's ability to create ex nihilo points to God's uniqueness. **3:27–28. that they would believe in Him**. Belief in God's reality is a natural quest of the human condition, built into the nature of Creation.

D'rash: 3:18. the Eternal, He is God. An exclamation of divine recognition, I Kings 18:39 reports that the Jewish people shouted this upon witnessing the victory of God over the priests of Baal. These words appear liturgically as one of the closing phrases of the entire High Holy Day period, uttered seven times in succession upon the conclusion of the Yom Kippur *N'ilah* service. **3:20. no corporeality.** This tenet appears as one of Maimonides' thirteen principles of faith. **3:20–21. lives and will not die.** God's eternality is implied by the Tetragrammaton (יהוה), a form of the verb "to be." **3:21–22. neither slumber nor sleep.** This phrase occurs in Psalm 121, describing God as the omnipresent Guardian of Israel. Not only is God above having to deal with bodily functions, such as sleeping and elimination of waste (when the priests of Baal fail to receive a response from their god during the contest on Mount Carmel, Elijah chides them by suggesting that Baal has either dozed off or is busy relieving himself), but divine omniscience and providence indicate that we can always turn to God. **3:26–28. He created…that they would believe in Him.** Rabbi Akiva states (*Pirkei Avot* 3:18): "Beloved is the human being, for he is created in God's image. It is indicative of a greater love that it was made known to him that he was created in God's image." Sforno comments that this teaching not only points to God's immanence, but to our ethical responsibilities toward our fellow humans as well. For we read in Genesis (9:5–6) of God's covenant with the children of Noah, "However, your blood that belongs to your souls, I will demand…for in the image of God He made the human being."

3:29 And when he raised his voice	וַיִּשָּׂא אֶת קוֹלוֹ
with these words, the idols that	בְּאֵלּוּ דְבָרִים וְהִנֵּה הַצְּלָמִים
3:31 were standing there fell on their	שֶׁהָיוּ שָׁם עוֹמְדִים נָפְלוּ עַל
faces. And when the king	פְּנֵיהֶם. וּכְרְאוֹת הַמֶּלֶךְ
3:33 and the ministers saw how they had fallen,	וְהַשָּׂרִים בְּמַפַּלְתָּם
and also [heard] the shouting	וְגַם צַעֲקַת
3:35 of Abraham, they fell on	אַבְרָהָם נָפְלוּ כֻלָּם עַל
their faces to the ground,	פְּנֵיהֶם אַרְצָה
3:37 including their king, Nimrod.	עִם מַלְכָּם נִמְרוֹד.
And he remained on the ground for	וְנִשְׁאַר
3:39 about two and a half hours.	כְּמוֹ שְׁתֵּי שָׁעוֹת וְחֵצִי אָרְצָה.
His [Nimrod's] heart melted within him.	וַיִּמַּס לִבּוֹ בְּקִרְבּוֹ,
3:41 His soul also took flight from him.	גַּם פָּרְחָה נִשְׁמָתוֹ מִמֶּנּוּ.

P'shat: 3:30–32. idols…fell on their faces. A sign of God's great power revealed for all to witness. **3:40. heart melted.** Nimrod's ego, his free will, dissolved. **3:41. His soul also took flight.** The soul leaving the body is a metaphor for death. Used here, it indicates God's might versus earthly (tyrannical) power.

D'rash: **3:31–32. fell on their faces.** This echoes the ancient Yom Kippur service of the Temple in Jerusalem. According to *Mishnah Yoma* 6:2, when the High Priest uttered the divine name, the power of the name caused all present to "fall upon their faces." **3:31–32. fell on their faces.** In Hebrew, the term for "word," דָּבָר (*davar*), also means "thing." Hence, we see how concrete the words of God's truth can be. The prayers we hear and utter on the High Holy Days possess the power to make the "idols" in our hearts "fall on their faces." **3:41. soul also took flight**. There are many examples of the use of this term in connection with the death of Sarah after hearing of the Binding of Isaac *(Akeidah),* thus forging an association with the New Year. *Pirkei D'Rabbi Eliezer,* chapter 32, states that before Sarah's soul took flight and left her, she emitted cries corresponding to the calls of the shofar.

3:42	And after two hours his breath	וְאַחַר שְׁתֵּי שָׁעוֹת שָׁב רוּחוֹ
	and his soul returned to his body	וְנִשְׁמָתוֹ אֶל גּוּפוֹ
3:44	and he awoke from his sleep.	וַיִּיקַץ מִשְּׁנָתוֹ,
	The king said, "Is this your voice	וַיֹּאמֶר הַמֶּלֶךְ, "הֲקוֹלְךָ זֶה
3:46	Abraham, or the voice of your	אַבְרָהָם אוֹ קוֹל
	God?"	אֱלֹהֶיךָ?"
3:48	He said to him, "This voice	וַיֹּאמֶר לוֹ, "קוֹל זֶה
	is the voice of the smallest of all the	קוֹל בְּרִיָּה קְטַנָּה מִכָּל
3:50	creatures that the Holy One	בְּרִיּוֹת שֶׁבָּרָא הַקָּדוֹשׁ,
	blessed be He created."	בָּרוּךְ הוּא."
3:52	At that moment King	בְּשָׁעָה הַהִיא אָמַר הַמֶּלֶךְ
	Nimrod said, "In truth, your God,	נִמְרוֹד, "בֶּאֱמֶת אֱלֹהֶיךָ
3:54	Abraham, is a great and	אַבְרָהָם אֱלוֹהַּ גָּדוֹל
	powerful God, the King of	וְחָזָק מֶלֶךְ מַלְכֵי
3:56	kings."	הַמְּלָכִים."
	And he said to Terach,	וְאָמַר לְתֶרַח
3:58	his father, that he should take his son	אָבִיו שֶׁיִּשָּׂא אֶת בְּנוֹ
	and remove him from his presence,	וְיָסַר מֵעָלָיו
3:60	and he should go to his city.	וַיֵּלֶךְ לְעִירוֹ.
	So the two of them went together.	וַיֵּלְכוּ שְׁנֵיהֶם יַחְדָּו.

P'shat: **3:49–50. the smallest of all the creatures.** This statement illustrates the humility of Abraham. **3:53. In truth**. Nimrod is legitimately moved by what he has experienced. **3:61. went together**. Terach was apparently also moved. He and his son entered the palace, disparate in motivation and consciousness. But, they left together united in their purpose.

26

3:61. went together. After his initial face-to-face confrontation with Nimrod, Abraham exits with his physical life assured (unlike the king, who has just been treated to a lesson in mortal vulnerability).

D'rash: 3:49–50. the smallest of all the creatures. R. Eliyahu HaCohein of Smyrna, the compiler of the *Shevet Musar,* states that he is publishing *Maaseh Avraham Avinu* in order to illustrate the great humility of Abraham. This aspect of the Patriarch's comport can serve as an example to us as we face the High Holy Day period. **3:53. In truth**. This episode echoes chapters 8–10 of the Book of Exodus, which describe how after Pharaoh acknowledges the power of God as exhibited through the plagues, wrought by the Almighty through His servant Moses, Pharaoh's heart is hardened and he stubbornly returns to his evil idolatrous ways. Here, although Nimrod acknowledges the power of God following the near-death experience wrought by God through His servant Abraham, the following episodes of the midrash illustrate that Nimrod also obstinately returns to his evil idolatrous ways. **3:60. his city**. The Torah (Genesis 11:31) identifies Abraham's birthplace as "Ur of the Chaldees." **3:61. went together**. The biblical account of the Binding of Isaac (the *Akeidah*), which is one of the Torah readings for Rosh HaShanah, twice states of Abraham and Isaac that "the two of them went together." In *Maaseh Avraham Avinu,* as well as the *Akeidah,* an encounter with God's Presence binds father and son. So, too, does the High Holy Day experience shine with the power to unite us and move us together along the path of righteousness.

GLEANINGS

Tikkun Olam

We believe that we can create a better world, and that we are an integral part of that act of *tikkun olam,* of creating a better world. Our tradition tells us that when God created the universe, one part of creation was left undone. That part was social justice....It is as if God said, "Here's the blueprint: the Torah. Here is the world that should be built, but now you must build it."

David Saperstein, "Mandate for Social Justice"

Copartners

...The Jewish passion for social justice had made a difference not only to Jews but to all the world. The refusal to yield to despair, fatigue, or cynicism; the stubborn belief in *tikkun olam* (repairing the world); the *chutzpadik* notion that we are copartners with God in refashioning a

humane and civilized world—these Jewish compulsions have helped preserve the Jewish spirit.

Albert Vorspan, *Start Worrying: Details to Follow*
(New York: UAHC Press, 1991), page 97

The Earthen Jar

The words of the Torah do not keep in one who is, in his own esteem, like a vessel of silver or of gold; but in one who is, in his own esteem, like the lowliest of vessels, an earthenware jar.

Midrash Tannaim 42

The Ten Steps

What is the greatest of the ten steps in the ascent of the righteous? Saintliness, as it is said: "Then you spoke in vision to your saints..." [Psalm 89:20]. Rabbi Y'hoshua ben Levi said: "Humility, for it is said, 'The spirit of the Eternal

God is upon me, to bring good tidings to the humble...' [Isaiah 61:1]. It does not say, 'to the saints,' but, 'to the humble,' from which we learn that humility is the greatest of all virtues."

Babylonian Talmud, Avodah Zarah 20b

Political Realities

In order to realize spiritual goals, we need to live in the world with our feet planted firmly on the ground. The promised land is not a blank canvas empty of human life, because a new community or a new nation isn't built in a vacuum. We have to work within the existing political realities. Though Abraham is a spiritual pioneer, he understands that he must navigate in the real world.

Naomi H. Rosenblatt and Joshua Horwitz, Wrestling with Angels (New York: Delta, 1995), page 103

Speaking Truth to Power

The Torah's plan for humanity concerns not only the development of righteous individuals, but the establishment of a model society based upon God's moral law. To this end, the text legislates forms of land management and ownership to remind people that their bounty comes from heaven and must be shared. Every year, farmers are to leave the corners of their fields unharvested so that the poor may glean. In the Sabbatical year, Scripture commands the farmer to neither sow nor harvest. What grows by itself must be shared by all: the farmer, the widow, the orphan, the stranger, even animals of the field. The Jubilee year calls for the return of all "sold" land to their original family owners, so that the majority of the land can never become the monopoly of the few. The priestly caste is not allowed to own land so that their power is held in check.

In this scheme, even the king is not above the law. The Scripture calls for a constitutional monarchy (if indeed the nation desires a king at all). The text requires the king to write his own Torah scroll and read from it publicly, at least once every seven years on Sukkot, the time when the most people would be in Jerusalem, the capital. This can be regarded as an illustration of the king's loyalty to the divine code.

The Torah also calls for a system of checks and balances. The prophet is called upon to ensure that the monarch and society in general live up to their mandates of ethical behavior and justice for all inhabitants of the land. Hence, the prophet's task involves reminding the government and society's power brokers of God's immutable moral law.

Examples of prophets speaking truth to power abound in the Bible. Samuel informs King Saul that he has lost God's favor for his refusal to follow divine commandment. Nathan chastises King David for the death of Bathsheba's husband, Uriah. Amos preaches against a society whose transgressions include selling the poor "for a pair of sandals." Jeremiah preaches the fall of Jerusalem as the consequence of sin.

All of these prophets share certain characteristics. At great risk to their personal safety, every one of these seers manifest the courage to confront those in power with their sins and inform them of the obligation, regardless of station, to live according to God's moral law. This is the same fortitude evident in the actions of Abraham in the midrash. Abraham confronts Nimrod, a human being who has placed himself above God's law, with the truth that he is only a person. And like all other people, he was created by the One God and is subject to divine power and morality.

Abraham's efforts aided in the spreading of God's influence, helping to make this world a better place. It is in this same tradition that Reform Judaism has emphasized the practice of social justice. We contain within us the ability to increase the Divine Presence on this earth, to heal the world through our strivings for what is moral and right. In the words of Rabbi David Saperstein, "To be a Jew means to be bound up with the struggle for social justice" ("Mandate for Social Justice").

During the 1960s, speaking truth to power meant fighting for the civil rights of all the inhabitants of the land. Today, there remain social ills no less egregious requiring that we as Jews speak out. In the tradition of Abraham and the great prophets of Israel, we are called upon to speak up and take action for the greater good, even if these ethical values are opposed by the rich and powerful. For it is only by taking a stand that we may realize the dream of centuries, the messianic vision of a world at peace, a model society ruled by justice and morality.

Chapter 4

T'shuvah: Idolatry and Spiritual Survival

While the first half of *Maaseh Avraham Avinu* addresses Abraham's survival against the threat of physical annihilation, as represented by Nimrod's murderous rampage directed against the male babies of Abraham's generation and the attack of the king's army upon the Patriarch, the remainder of the midrash depicts the Patriarch in danger of spiritual destruction. In this chapter, Abraham finds himself in the position of working for his father, Terach, in the family business of idol manufacture and sales.

Abraham's efforts to remain true to his divinely ordained destiny amidst an idolatrous world reveal not only what it means to be God's servant, but point to God's uniqueness. The episode concerning the old woman who initially seeks to purchase an idol illustrates the ever-present possibility of *t'shuvah*.

This story is not just Abraham's, but our own. There is a rabbinic saying that the deeds of the Patriarchs are repeated by their children. Like Abraham, we must test our spiritual values against a vast secular landscape far more enamored of material wealth than the riches of religious heritage and practice. We are further challenged, as was Abraham, by virtue of our distinct minority status as Jews. Abraham's struggles amidst a non-Jewish world are similar to our own. Many of us face situations in which the demands of work are pitted against our religious aspirations. Even being able to take time off in order to attend High Holy Day services can sometimes prove difficult.

Abraham's family situation may ring true as well. Many of us may have chosen paths that differ from those of our parents. For many, the reclaiming of Jewish tradition means spells of walking a hard road of separation from the values and ways of our families. My announcement at the age of eleven that I wanted to become a rabbi and lead a religious life earned me a checkup with a psychologist. Abraham's quests for identity and integrity within the context of his family as presented in this upcoming episode may feel very familiar.

As with previous chapters, the text presents what may be considered another test for Abraham. Once again, the Patriarch proves equal to the task at hand. In a now familiar pattern, the chapter begins with a challenge and moves to praise of the Holy One.

4:1 It happened after this that	וַיְהִי אַחֲרֵי כֵן,
Abraham reached the age of	וַיִּגְדַּל אַבְרָהָם עַד שֶׁהָיָה כְּבֶן
4:3 twenty years old, and Terach, his	עֶשְׂרִים שָׁנָה וְתֶרַח
father, became sick. He said to	אָבִיו חָלָה. וַיֹּאמֶר אֶל
4:5 his sons, Haran and Abraham,	בָּנָיו הָרָן וְאַבְרָהָם,
"By your lives, my sons, sell these	"בְּחַיֵּיכֶם בָּנַי, תִּמְכְּרוּ אֵלּוּ
4:7 two idols, because I don't have	שְׁנֵי צְלָמִים שֶׁאֵין לִי
money to pay for our expenses."	מָעוֹת לְהוֹצָאוֹתֵינוּ."
4:9 Haran went and sold the idols	הָלַךְ הָרָן וּמָכַר אֶת הַצְּלָמִים
and brought the monies to cover	וְהֵבִיא מָעוֹת
4:11 his father's expenses.	לְהוֹצָאוֹת אָבִיו.

P'shat: 4:6–7. sell these two idols. Terach made his living as a fashioner and purveyor of idolatrous statues, and he brought his sons into the business. **4:9. Haran went and sold**. The term "went" may be understood to indicate Haran's willingness and enthusiasm in selling the idols. The text will contrast Haran's behavior with that of his brother, Abraham. This again points to the strength of Abraham's faith and resolve in serving the One God.

D'rash: 4:6–7. sell these two idols. The tradition that Terach was an idolater is apparently of ancient origin. In Joshua 24:2 we read, "Your fathers dwelt of old time beyond the River, even Terach, the father of Abraham, the father of Nachor, and they served other gods." The *Amora* Rav felt that this verse should begin the *Magid* section of the Passover Haggadah, as it effectively compares the ignominy of slavery to the degradation of idolatry. **4:9. Haran went and sold**. *B'reishit Rabbah* depicts Haran as a man torn between two positions and loyalties. When Nimrod throws Abraham into the fiery furnace, Haran merely stands by. "If Abraham is victorious," he thinks, "I shall say that I am of Abraham's belief, while if Nimrod wins out, I will pledge to be on Nimrod's side." Haran witnesses that Abraham descends into the furnace but is saved. Therefore, when Nimrod asks him, "Of whose belief are you?" he replies, "Of Abraham's." Immediately Nimrod casts Haran into the furnace. His innards are burned, and he dies. Haran's lack of true faith and conviction is shown to cause his downfall, his burning a metaphor for being consumed by an idolatrous society. We, like Haran, become susceptible to the destructive fires of the materialistic society that surrounds us when our dedication to Judaism and faith in God's commandments grow weak. One reason we come to the synagogue on the High Holy Days is to strengthen one another by sharing those experiences that reinforce our trust in God's moral law, our commitment to Judaism, and our resolve to do good in the world.

31

4:12	Abraham went and took two other	וַיֵּלֶךְ אַבְרָהָם וַיִּקַּח שְׁנֵי
	idols to sell. He put a rope around	צְלָמִים אֲחֵרִים לְמָכְרָם, וְשָׂם חֶבֶל עַל
4:14	their throats and put their faces to	גְּרוֹנָם וּפְנֵיהֶם
	the ground, and he dragged them	אָרְצָה, וְהוּא הָיָה סוֹכֵב אוֹתָם
4:16	and shouted, "Who wants to buy	וְצוֹעֵק וְאָמַר, "מִי הוּא זֶה שִׁיקָנֶה
	an idol that serves no purpose,	צֶלֶם שֶׁאֵין בּוֹ תּוֹעֶלֶת,
4:18	neither to itself nor to one who	לֹא לְעַצְמוֹ וְלֹא לְמִי
	would buy it in order to worship it?	שִׁיקָנֵהוּ לְעוֹבְדוֹ?
4:20	And it has a mouth, but will not	וְגַם יֵשׁ לוֹ פֶּה וְלֹא
	speak; an eye, but will not see;	יְדַבֵּר, עַיִן וְלֹא יִרְאֶה,
4:22	legs, but will not walk; an ear,	רַגְלַיִם וְלֹא יֵלֵךְ, אֹזֶן
	but will not hear."	וְלֹא יִשְׁמַע."

P'shat: 4:15. he dragged them. In biblical parlance, "dragging" is seen as a punishment for sin, especially for those who cause others to sin. For example, we read in Jeremiah 22:19 of the evil King Jehoiakim, "He shall be buried with the burial of an ass, dragged and cast forth beyond the gates of Jerusalem." At this juncture of the midrash, Abraham's dragging of the idols through the streets of Babylon serves as the perfect counterpoint to the king's earlier having led through the streets with honor those who performed his idolatrous bidding.

D'rash: 4:15–16. he dragged them and shouted. Again, Abraham's foray through the public spaces of Babylon, shouting God's message, is reminiscent of Jonah's prophetic mission to Nineveh. As we read in Jonah 3:4–5, "Jonah began going through the city one day's journey, and he proclaimed and said, 'In another forty days Nineveh will be overthrown.' And the people of Nineveh believed in God." The actions of both Abraham and Jonah are reminders of the mission of Israel to spread the blessings of ethical monotheism to the world. This sense of the mission of Israel is a central theme of Rosh HaShanah, as the New Year marks the anniversary of Creation, a clearly universal event. In the *K'dushat HaYom* section of the High Holy Day *T'filah,* we pray וְתֵן פַּחְדְּךָ עַל כָּל מַעֲשֶׂיךָ (*v'tein p'chd'cha al kol maasecha*), "and place Your reverence in all that You have made," indicating our responsibilities toward all the peoples of the earth.

4:24	And when the people of the	וּכְשָׁמוֹעַ אַנְשֵׁי
	country heard the words of	הַמְּדִינָה אֶת דִּבְרֵי
4:26	Abraham, our Patriarch,	אַבְרָהָם אָבִינוּ,
	may he rest in peace,	עָלָיו הַשָּׁלוֹם,

they were very surprised.	תָּמְהוּ עַד מְאֹד.
4:28 While he was walking,	וְהוּא הוֹלֵךְ
he met an old woman, and she	וּבָא וּפָגַע זְקֵנָה אַחַת
4:30 said to him, "By your life	וַתֹּאמֶר לוֹ, "בְּחַיֶּיךָ
Abraham, choose for me	אַבְרָהָם תִּבְחַר לִי
4:32 a very good and large idol	צֶלֶם אֶחָד טוֹב עַד מְאֹד וְגָדוֹל
to worship and to love."	לְעוֹבְדוֹ וּלְאַהֲבוֹ."

P'shat: **4:27. very surprised.** The people of the country listen, and Abraham's words of truth have effect. **4:32. large idol.** One can extrapolate that the old woman assumes that the larger the idol, the more powerful it will be. The text here subtly compares this kind of concrete and primitive thought with the abstract logic with which the idea of faith in the One God is approached. **4:33. to worship and to love.** The author here employs terms (אַהֲבָה *[ahavah]*, love; and עֲבוֹדָה *[avodah]*, worship) associated with Jewish prayer and the Jewish individual's duties toward God. The old woman's application of these terms with reference to a large idol illustrates the extent of her misplaced reverence and underscores God's uniqueness. The combination of "love" and "worship" should be reserved for the one being for whom it is appropriate, God.

D'rash: **4:27. very surprised.** Just as words prove to be the effective medium of Abraham's message of truth, High Holy Day services and Torah study consist of many words. If we allow ourselves to hear these words of truth, perhaps we will be surprised at their effect upon us. It is one thing to go through the words, quite another to allow the words to go through us. **4:29. met an old woman.** Various versions of Abraham's encounters with prospective idol buyers exist (see the gleanings at the end of the chapter). In all of these versions, Abraham invariably applies logic, the same method that our midrash depicts the Patriarch using to discover the One God in the first place. Thus, the text teaches that logic can bring us to knowledge of the One God as can revelatory religious experience. **4:33. to worship and to love.** Numerous examples of the commandments to love and worship God may be found in the Bible. Among these, Deuteronomy 6:5–9, "You shall love the Eternal, your God," and Deuteronomy 11:13–21, "to love the Eternal, your God, and to serve [worship] Him with all your heart and all your soul" have traditionally found central places in our liturgy as part of the *Sh'ma* rubric.

4:34 He said to her, "Old woman,	אָמַר לָהּ, "זְקֵנָה,
old woman, I don't know	זְקֵנָה אֵינִי יוֹדֵעַ
4:36 of any usefulness in them;	בָּהֶם תּוֹעֶלֶת
not in a large one, nor a small one,	לֹא בְּגָדוֹל וְלֹא בְּקָטָן,

33

4:38	neither for themselves, nor	לֹא לְעַצְמָם וְלֹא
	for others."	לַאֲחֵרִים."
4:40	He [further] said to her,	אָמַר לָהּ,
	"The large idol that you bought	"וְהַצֶּלֶם הַגָּדוֹל אֲשֶׁר לָקַחַתְּ
4:42	from my brother, Haran, to worship,	מֵאָחִי הָרָן לְעָבְדוֹ,
	what happened to it?"	הֵיכָן הָלַךְ?"
4:44	She said to him, "Thieves	אָמְרָה לוֹ, "בָּאוּ גַנָּבִים
	came that [fateful] night	בַּלַּיְלָה הַהוּא
4:46	and stole it while I was still	וְגָנְבוּ אוֹתוֹ בְּעוֹדִי
	in the bathhouse."	בְּבֵית הַמֶּרְחָץ."

P'shat: 4:47. in the bathhouse. The Talmud associates the term "bathhouse" with the practice of idolatry and, hence, immorality. In ancient days, bathhouses were built by the Romans and frequently contained statues associated with the Greco-Roman pantheon. The fact that the old woman's property was stolen while she was still in the bathhouse points to a milieu of immorality. As we read in *Pirkei Avot* 4:2, "Ben Azzai said: 'One sin leads to another.'"

D'rash: 4:47. in the bathhouse. Babylonian Talmud, *B'rachot* 60a (the tractate that deals with prayer) presents a prayer to be said upon entering and leaving a bathhouse. Upon entering, the Jew prays that "no humiliation or iniquity befall me." When leaving, the text reports in the name of Rabbi Acha, one should thank God for having "delivered me from the fire." The implication here is that as long as we live in a world yet unredeemed, we are, in effect, unavoidably bathed in potentially harmful influences. The waters of such influence may affect us as does the destructiveness of a consuming fire. Our clinging to God and the ways of righteousness, however, can act as purifying protection. In chapter 6 of this volume, the midrash directly compares the effects of an idolatrous society to the destructiveness of fire, as King Nimrod builds a fiery furnace in an effort to immolate Abraham and eradicate his influence.

4:48	He said to her, "If this is so,	אָמַר לָהּ, "אִם כֵּן,
	how could you serve the idol?	כֵּיצַד תַּעַבְדִי לְצֶלֶם?
4:50	It could not even save itself	כִּי אַף לְעַצְמוֹ לֹא הִצִּיל
	from the thieves; all the more	מִן הַגַּנָּבִים, כָּל שֶׁכֵּן
4:52	so will it not save others	שֶׁלֹּא יַצִּיל לַאֲחֵרִים
	from their evil. And it will not save	מֵרָעָתָם. וְלֹא אֶת

4:54	you, foolish old woman!	הַזְּקֵנָה הַשׁוֹטָה!
	And how, tell me, can the idol	וְכֵיצַד תֹּאמְרִי שֶׁהַצֶּלֶם
4:56	that you served be God? [If it is God,]	שֶׁעָבַדְתְּ שֶׁהוּא אֱלוֹהַ
	why did it not save itself from	לָמָה לֹא הִצִּיל אֶת עַצְמוֹ מִן
4:58	the hand of thieves? Rather, it is	הַגַּנָּבִים? אֶלָּא שֶׁהוּא
	an idol that has no purpose,	צֶלֶם שֶׁאֵין בּוֹ תּוֹעֶלֶת
4:60	not for itself, nor for one who	לֹא לְעַצְמוֹ וְלֹא לְמִי
	would worship it."	שֶׁיַּעֲבוֹד אוֹתוֹ."
4:62	The old woman said to him,	אָמְרָה לוֹ הַזְּקֵנָה,
	"If this is as you say, Abraham,	"אִם כֵּן אַבְרָהָם כִּדְבָרֶיךָ
4:64	whom should I serve?"	לְמִי אֶעֱבוֹד?"

P'shat: **4:50. could not even save.** God's ability to save, as opposed to the ineffectiveness of idols, may be seen as an aspect of God's uniqueness.

D'rash: **4:50. could not even save.** The divine power to save is an especially poignant idea during the High Holy Day period. Jewish tradition regards the Days of Awe as a time of judgment during which God declares and seals our fates for the coming year. It is by turning to God and serving the Holy One in prayer, intention, and deed that we can be saved from evil. As we declare in the *Un'taneh Tokef* of the High Holy Day liturgy: "But repentance, prayer, and charity temper judgment's severe decree." (See pages 109 and 314 of *Gates of Repentance.*) It should be noted that many liberal Jews regard this aspect in the metaphoric sense. Rather than an image of God as literally sitting in heaven reviewing a ledger during the Ten Days of Repentance and making notations as to who will live and who will die in the coming year, instead this idea serves to remind us that our actions cannot escape divine scrutiny. Our deeds bear consequences for our own lives and the world around us. Repentance, prayer, and charity "temper judgment's severe decree" by adding depth to our lives and helping spread the influence of God's morality in the world.

4:66	He said to her, "Serve the	אָמַר לָהּ, "תַּעַבְדִי
	God of gods; the Lord of	לֵאלֹהֵי הָאֱלֹהִים וַאֲדוֹנֵי
4:68	lords; the Creator of heaven	הָאֲדוֹנִים, בּוֹרֵא שָׁמַיִם
	and earth, them and all that is in them;	וָאָרֶץ, הַיָּם וְכָל אֲשֶׁר בָּם.
4:70	and He is the God of	וְהוּא אֱלֹהֵי
	Nimrod; and the God of Terach;	נִמְרוֹד וֵאלֹהֵי תֶּרַח
4:72	and God of east, west, south,	וֵאלֹהֵי מִזְרָח וּמַעֲרָב, דָּרוֹם
	and north. And who is	וְצָפוֹן. וּמִי

4:74 Nimrod? The dog who would

make himself a god so that

4:76 others would worship him."

נִמְרוֹד? הַכֶּלֶב

שֶׁיַּעֲשֶׂה עַצְמוֹ אֱלוֹהַ

לַעֲבֹד אוֹתוֹ!"

P'shat: 4:68–69. Creator of heaven and earth. The universal God. **4:70–71. God of Nimrod; and the God of Terach.** Even those who would deny God's reality and/or power are still subject to the truth of God's existence and influence. **4:72–73. east, west, south, and north.** This again may be seen as a statement of God's effective power to save. Psalm 107:2–3 praises God for having redeemed His people "from the hand of the tormenter and gathered them out of the lands, from the east and from the west, from the north and from the sea." The *Targum* adds the word "southern" before "sea." **4:74. dog.** Despite the animal's modern-day popularity, the term "dog" in the Bible as well as rabbinic literature bears a negative connotation. In the ancient Near East, dogs would prowl about towns in half-wild condition, living on offal and garbage. **4:75. make himself a god.** This parallels the tradition that the Pharaoh of the Exodus also declared himself a god. Historically, the Syrian-Greek king Antiochus and the Roman emperor Caligula, both persecutors of the Jewish people, declared themselves gods.

D'rash: 4:68–69. Creator of heaven and earth. The universal nature of God is one of the central themes of Rosh HaShanah, regarded as the birthday of the world, the anniversary of Creation. This theme is attested to liturgically in the Shofar Service. **4:70–71. God of Nimrod; and the God of Terach.** The structure of the sentence resembles Jewish liturgical form. The *Avot* (page 30 of *Gates of Repentance*) begins: "Praised be our God, the God of our fathers and mothers: God of Abraham, God of Isaac, God of Jacob. . . ." The Rabbis ask why each of the Patriarchs is mentioned separately, instead of "God of Abraham, Isaac, and Jacob." They answer that God was manifested in the life of each Patriarch in a unique fashion, for each maintained a unique, personal relationship with the Divine. The midrash contrasting the names of Nimrod and Terach with those of the Patriarchs serves as a reminder that each of us is capable of establishing a unique personal relationship with God. The High Holy Days are a period when we examine our relationships, not only with those around us and with ourselves, but also with God. **4:74. dog.** *Midrash HaGadol* pictures the nations of the world as a dog, too ethically weak and too wild and undisciplined to support the burden of Torah and mitzvot, or even the seven Noachide commandments. In the eyes of the midrash, the responsibility of spreading morality to the world and sharing God's kindness falls squarely upon the shoulders of Jews. This mission is an aspect of what it means to be God's servant, and aspiring to fulfill this mission constitutes a resolution to do better in the New Year. **4:76. others would worship.** The connection between the midrash and the story of the Exodus is further attested to by the appearance of the term לַעֲבֹד *(laavod),* which can mean both "to worship" and "to serve." Interestingly, the Torah utilizes this same verb in relation to Pharaoh and the Egyptians, as well as in connection with God. When used in reference to human beings, "service" equals "slavery," as we read in Exodus 1:13: וַיַּעֲבִדוּ מִצְרַיִם אֶת בְּנֵי יִשְׂרָאֵל (vayaavdu Mitzrayim et b'nei Yisrael), "The Egyptians made the Children of Israel serve," or better, "The Egyptians enslaved the Children of Israel." When describing our relationship with God, however, the Torah indicates a service of love (Deuteronomy 11:13): לְאַהֲבָה אֶת יי אֱלֹהֵיכֶם וּלְעָבְדוֹ (l'ahavah et Adonai Eloheichem u'l'ovdo), "to love the Eternal your God and to serve Him." In fact, in its noun form, avodah (עֲבוֹדָה) stands for the Jewish worship service. Indeed, attending worship services in the synagogue can be thought of as a demonstration of a loving relationship with the Divine. But the appropriation of reverence where it duly belongs may be made in other ways as well. Every time one performs an act of loving-kindness for another human being, studies Torah, upholds the cause of justice in the world, gives *tzedakah*, behaves in such a way as to bring others to bless the Holy One, or observes any mitzvah, it is considered divine service. The decision to rededicate ourselves to love and serve God that emerges from the process of High Holy Day introspection can reverberate throughout the year.

4:77	The old woman said,	אָמְרָה הַזְּקֵנָה,
	"From now on I will not serve	"מִכָּאן וּלְהַלָּן לֹא אֶעֱבוֹד
4:79	anyone except your God, the	כִּי אִם אֱלֹהֶיךָ
	God of Abraham. And if I serve	אֱלֹהֵי אַבְרָהָם. וְאִם אֶעֱבוֹד
4:81	Him, what benefit will there be	אוֹתוֹ מַה תּוֹעֶלֶת יִהְיֶה
	for me?"	לִי?"
4:83	He said to her, "Everything	אָמַר לָהּ, "כָּל
	that they stole will be returned	מַה שֶּׁגָּנְבוּ יָשׁוּב
4:85	to you, and also your soul will be saved	לָךְ וְגַם תַּצִּיל נַפְשֵׁךְ
	from *Geihinnom*."	מִגֵּיהִנָּם."
4:87	The old woman said to	אָמְרָה הַזְּקֵנָה,
	him, "What shall I say in order	"מָה אוֹמֵר כְּדֵי
4:89	to save my soul from	לְהַצִּיל אֶת נַפְשִׁי
	destruction?"	מִשַּׁחַת?"
4:91	He said to her, "Say,	אָמַר לָהּ, "תֹּאמְרִי:
	'The Lord, He is God in the heavens	יי הוּא הָאֱלֹהִים בַּשָּׁמַיִם
4:93	above and the earth below;	מִמַּעַל וְעַל הָאָרֶץ מִתַּחַת,
	He is One, there is none other.'"	אֶחָד וְאֵין שֵׁנִי."

P'shat: **4:83–84. Everything that they stole.** There are material benefits to serving the one true God. **4:85. your soul will be saved.** Spiritual benefits accrue from one's service to God. **4:86. Geihinnom.** Literally, the "Valley of Hinnom." Archaeologists have discovered the charred remains of children, victims of idolatrous human sacrifice, in this valley just outside of Jerusalem. The term has become synonymous with "hell."

D'rash: 4:83–84. Everything that they stole. Following God's commandments will bring peace and, hence, material prosperity; as we read in Deuteronomy 11:13–15, "If you will hearken to my commandments…I shall provide rain for your land in its proper time, the early and the late rains, that you may gather in your grain, your wine, and your oil. I shall provide grass in your field for your cattle, and you will eat and you will be satisfied." **4:85. your soul will be saved.** Service to God can save one's soul from the curses of insensitivity to the needs of others and ignorance of the spiritual joys of love. **4:86. *Geihinnom*.** Rabbinic literature relates many varied images of *Geihinnom*. Among them is *Sh'mot Rabbah* 7:4, which regards it as a place of weeping and fires, where only the wicked will be consigned following their earthly sojourns.

4:95	"'He brings death and gives life;	‏"מֵמִית וּמְחַיֶּה,
	He lives and will not see death;	‏הוּא חַי וְלֹא יִרְאֶה מָוֶת
4:97	and also that I, Abraham,	‏וְגַם אֲנִי אַבְרָהָם
	am the trusted servant of His house.'"	‏עַבְדּוֹ נֶאֱמָן בֵּיתוֹ."
4:99	The old woman said,	‏אָמְרָה הַזְּקֵנָה,
	"From now on I will declare	‏"מִכָּאן וּלְהַלָּן אֲנִי אוֹמֶרֶת
4:101	these words of yours,	‏כִּדְבָרֶיךָ,
	and I will attest that the Lord, He is	‏וְאָעִיד עַל עַצְמִי שֵׁיי הוּא
4:103	God in the heavens above and	‏הָאֱלֹהִים בַּשָּׁמַיִם מִמַּעַל
	the earth below, and you are	‏וְעַל הָאָרֶץ מִתַּחַת, וְאַתָּה
4:105	Abraham, His prophet."	‏אַבְרָהָם נְבִיאוֹ."

P'shat: 4:95. gives life. This statement points to God's uniqueness, as no other being is capable of creating life, certainly not an idol. **4:96. will not see death.** Eternality is an aspect of God's uniqueness. **4:102. I will attest.** Bearing witness to the One God by reciting certain words has long been part of the Jewish liturgical tradition. **4:102–103. He is God.** Religious experience leads to faith.

D'rash: 4:95. brings death and gives life. This phrase receives liturgical expression in the *Amidah* prayer, which is repeated at least three times daily. Specifically, the phrase is part of the *Amidah*'s second blessing, praising God's might and power. The divine control of all life looms especially important during the High Holy Day period, a time of heavenly judgment. The mention of God's mastery over life and death also bears the ethical prescription that only God and God alone is fit to make and implement such decisions over life and death.

4:102. I will attest. The *Sh'ma* (שְׁמַע יִשְׂרָאֵל יי אֱלֹהֵינוּ יי אֶחָד, [Sh'ma Yisrael Adonai Eloheinu Adonai Echad], "Hear, O Israel: the Eternal is our God, the Eternal is One"), which occupies a central place in our liturgy, is the ultimate verbal attestation to God's existence and unity. It is not surprising then that the closing ceremony of the High Holy Days (N'ilah) also features these words.

4:106	"And I will believe in the Lord, may He be blessed,	"וְאַאֲמִין בַּיי יִתְבָּרַךְ
4:108	and in you." The Maggid said that she repented	וּבְךְ." אָמַר הַמַּגִּיד שֶׁשָּׁבָה
4:110	and regretted having served the idols. And they said	בִּתְשׁוּבָה וְנִתְחָרְטָה עַל שֶׁעָבְדָה אֶת הַצְּלָמִים. וְאָמְרוּ
4:112	that she even found the thieves and they returned to	שֶׁגַּם מָצְאָה הַגַּנָּבִים וְהֵשִׁיבוּ
4:114	her all the stolen property, including the idol. What did	לָה כָּל מַה שֶּׁגָּנְבוּ וְגַם הַצֶּלֶם. מָה
4:116	this old woman do? She took a stone in her hand and hit the	עָשְׂתָה זֹאת הַזְּקֵנָה? לָקְחָה אֶבֶן בְּיָדָהּ וְהִכְּתָה
4:118	idol's head, saying, "Woe to you and to whomever shall	עַל רֹאשׁ הַצֶּלֶם וְאוֹמֶרֶת, "אוֹי לָךְ וּלְמִי
4:120	serve you in the future. For you have no purpose, and give none	שֶׁיַּעֲבוֹד אוֹתְךְ עוֹד. כִּי אֵין בָּךְ תּוֹעֶלֶת וְלֹא
4:122	to one who would serve you."	לְמִי שֶׁיַּעֲבוֹד אוֹתְךְ."

P'shat: **4:115–116. What did this old woman do?** The old woman's behavior can be seen as constituting a conversion to true religion.

D'rash: **4:106. I will believe.** This parallels Exodus 14:31, which states that after having experienced God's salvation at the Reed Sea, "...they believed in God, and in Moses, His servant." **4:109. she repented.** The repentance of the idolatrous old woman illustrates that *t'shuvah* and change are ever possible and that they can be approached through a liturgical religious experience. For more on *t'shuvah,* see the gleanings at the conclusion of this chapter. **4:109–110 she...regretted.** Our tradition regards regret for past wrongdoing as an essential step on the road to *t'shuvah* and self-improvement. This is why Elul, the month preceding the Days of Awe, is regarded as one of introspection or *cheshbon hanefesh,* literally, "an accounting of the soul." It is this inner examination that leads to regret for those shortcomings that have prevented us from achieving our true God-given potentials. The regret, in turn, propels us to make restitution for the wrongs we have done, to effectively turn to our higher selves and, hence, behave in improved fashion in the New Year. **4:115–116. What did this old woman do?** *B'reishit Rabbah* 39:14 interprets Genesis 12:5, "... and the souls they made in Charan...," to indicate that Abraham made converts. Rashi comments that since he brought others beneath the wings of God's Presence (the *Shechinah*), Scripture praises him by indicating that it is as if Abraham had "made" them, in essence, that he created them. Thus we see that what it means to be God's servant involves being God's partner in Creation, not only in the physical sense of propagating the species, but in acts of spiritual encouragement and guidance as well. According to Rashi's reading of the midrash, Abraham served as a kind of ancient Outreach committee chairperson.

4:124 And she went forth	וַיְצֵאָה
from her house into the markets and	מִבֵּיתָהּ בַּשּׁוּקִים
4:126 town squares, and she shouted,	בָּרְחוֹבוֹת וְהִיא צוֹעֶקֶת
saying, "Anyone who wants	וְאוֹמֶרֶת, "מִי שֶׁרוֹצֶה
4:128 to save his soul	לְהַצִּיל נַפְשׁוֹ
from destruction and be successful	מִשַּׁחַת וְיַצְלִיחַ
4:130 in everything he does, let him	בְּכָל מַעֲשָׂיו
serve the God of Abraham."	וַעֲבוֹד לֵאלֹהֵי אַבְרָהָם."
4:132 The Maggid said	אָמַר הַמַּגִּיד
that every day this old woman	שֶׁהַזְּקֵנָה בְּכָל יוֹם
4:134 would shout until many men and	הָיְתָה צוֹעֶקֶת עַד שֶׁהֵשִׁיבָה
women repented.	בִּתְשׁוּבָה אֲנָשִׁים וְנָשִׁים הַרְבֵּה.

P'shat: **4:124. she went forth**. The old woman's faith propels her to righteous action. It is not enough to simply know the truth, rather one must act on it, sharing deeds of truth with others.

D'rash: **4:124. she went forth**. The old woman's behavior is not only imitative of Abraham's, but is reminiscent of Jonah's in the book that bears his name (the haftarah for the afternoon of Yom Kippur). In both instances, public proclamations lead to *t'shuvah*. Our own public calls to repentance and statements of faith during the religious services of the Days of Awe have a similar power to turn us toward the path of good. **4:126. she shouted**. The old woman's shouts roused repentance among those who heard her. In this way, her shouts may be compared to the voice of the shofar, which Maimonides depicts as saying to us: "Wake up from your deep sleep, you who are fast asleep... search your deeds and repent; remember your Creator... examine your souls, mend your ways and deeds. Let everyone give up his evil ways and bad plans." **4:129. be successful**. Many of our prayers contain pleas for the "success of our hands," in other words, the prosperity to meet our earthly needs. For instance, Psalm 118, read as part of the *Hallel* (literally, "Praise") rubric, implores: "Please God, bring success now!" Such a prayer is an act of humility, for it acknowledges that our wealth ultimately does not only depend upon our own talents and efforts, but upon the Ruler of the universe. **4:134–135. men and women repented.** Repentance in Jewish tradition implies behavioral changes, not just verbal statements. Our resolutions and good intentions must manifest themselves in a change for the better in terms of comportment in order to be considered true *t'shuvah*. This principle is illustrated in the Book of Jonah. What causes God to turn back from raining punishment upon the Ninevites is that the people were "turning back from their evil ways" (Jonah 3:10). Hence, the Talmud emphasizes: "The verse does not read, 'God saw their sackcloth and their fasting,' but 'God saw what they did, how they were turning back from their evil ways'" (Babylonian Talmud, *Taanit* 16a).

4:136	The king heard news of her	שָׁמַע הַמֶּלֶךְ שְׁמוּעָה זֹאת
	and he sent for her	וְשָׁלַח אַחֲרֶיהָ
4:138	and brought her before him.	וְהֶבִיאוּהָ לְפָנָיו.
	He said to her, "What have you	אָמַר לָהּ, "מַה זֹאת
4:140	done that you have mocked	עָשִׂית כִּי שָׁטִית
	my service behind my back?	מֵאַחֲרֵי עֲבוֹדָתִי?
4:142	Why will you not serve me,	לָמָה לֹא תַּעַבְדִי אוֹתִי
	for I am your god? And I have	שֶׁאֲנִי אֱלֹהֵיךְ? וְאֲנִי
4:144	formed you,	יְצַרְתִּיךְ
	I have even supported you	אַף תְּמַכְתִּיךְ
4:146	with my right hand."	בִּימִינִי."
	She answered, saying,	הֵשִׁיבָה וְאָמְרָה,
4:148	"You are one of the liars.	"אַתָּה מִן הַכּוֹזְבִים
	And you are a denier of the	וְאַתָּה כּוֹפֵר
4:150	principle of	בְּעִיקָר
	'There is one God and none other!'"	אֵל אֶחָד וְאֵין שֵׁנִי!"

P'shat: **4:143. I am your god.** Merely "hearing" the truth is obviously not enough. Like the Pharaoh of the Exodus, Nimrod remains unmoved. His claim to have "formed" the old woman is another glaring example of his deluded arrogance. For only the true Creator, the One God, acts as the "former" of human beings. **4:146. my right hand.** The "right hand" in biblical parlance connotes redemption. For instance, Psalm 118:15–16 offers the following praise for God's support and deliverance: "The right hand of the Eternal does valiantly. The right hand of the Eternal is exalted."

41

D'rash: 4:143–144. I have formed you. The idea of "forming" as a unique and godly act of Creation is expressed liturgically in the *Asher Yatzar* blessing, recited daily as part of the Morning Blessings and also recited upon emerging from the bathroom: "Blessed are You, O Eternal our God, Sovereign of the universe, who has formed a human being with wisdom and created within him [a wondrous network of many] openings and hollows." The idea of God purposefully creating and forming us imbues our actions with a sense of divinely charged mission.

4:152 "And you eat	"וְאַתָּה אוֹכֵל
from His goodness, but you would	מִטּוּבוֹ
4:154 worship another;	וְתַעֲבוֹד אֵל אַחֵר
and you would deny Him,	וְתִכְפּוֹר בּוֹ
4:156 and His Torah, and Abraham,	וְתוֹרָתוֹ וְאַבְרָהָם
His servant."	עַבְדּוֹ."
4:158 And when the king heard	וַיְהִי כִּשְׁמוֹעַ הַמֶּלֶךְ
her words, he gave the command	אֶת דְּבָרֶיהָ צִוָּה
4:160 to kill her.	לַהֲרוֹג אוֹתָהּ,
They killed her, but he, in his heart,	וַיַּהַרְגוּ אוֹתָהּ.
4:162 became afraid but defiant on	וּפָחַד וְרָהַב לְבָבוֹ
account of her words.	מִדְּבָרֶיהָ.
4:164 And he was surprised at himself,	וְתָמַהּ עַל עַצְמוֹ
for he didn't know what he would do	וְלֹא יָדַע מַה יַּעֲשֶׂה
4:166 with Abraham,	עִם אַבְרָהָם
who had caused the loss of [the	שֶׁהִפְסִיד
4:168 people's] faith in him; for the	אֱמוּנָתוֹ. כִּי
majority of the multitudes of the	רוֹב הֲמוֹן הָעָם
4:170 people believed in the God of	הֶאֱמִינוּ בֵּאלֹהֵי
Abraham.	אַבְרָהָם.

P'shat: 4:152–153. eat from His goodness. This phrase echoes the Blessing after Meals, which states that God "feeds the world through His goodness." **4:154. worship another**. "Namely, yourself, your own ambition, and even your own image." **4:156. His Torah**. Although this episode chronologically precedes the giving of the Torah at Sinai, Jewish tradition has it that God actually created the Torah before He created the world and used it as a blueprint for Creation and that an aspect of Abraham's greatness lay in his observance of all of its precepts. Alternately, the term *torato* (תּוֹרָתוֹ) may be used in the generic sense of

"His teachings." **4:159–160. command to kill her**. Nimrod's power is limited to his ability to destroy. But even his killing of the old woman cannot silence her message, the news of God's goodness.

D'rash: 4:152–153. eat from His goodness. *B'reishit Rabbah* 54:6 depicts the Blessing after Meals as central to Abraham's mission. Once wayfarers had enjoyed the Patriarch's hospitality and had eaten to satisfaction, Abraham would teach them the Blessing after Meals. Thus, according to *B'reishit Rabbah,* did the Patriarch bring many in his day to the recognition of God and the practice of true religion. By extension, we hope that our own utterances of thanksgiving will lead us to a deeper perception of God's role in our lives and impel us to righteous behavior. **4:156. His Torah**. God's "Teachings" represent the divine prescription for the moral equilibrium of the individual and the world. Nimrod's sins are not necessarily theological. Rather, his behaviors present the arrant problem. **4:159–160. command to kill her**. The old woman displayed amazing courage in standing up to the immorality of her age, as represented by the bloodthirsty King Nimrod, despite great risk to herself personally. Her martyrdom is reminiscent of the fate and faith of the ten great Jewish scholars whom the Roman emperor Hadrian murdered circa 135 C.E. for the crimes of association with the Bar Kochba rebellion and the teaching of Torah. This tale of the ten comprises part of the Yom Kippur service. Our spiritual lives often seem to be threatened by Nimrod-like forces that inhabit our everyday landscape, that is, the demands upon us of work and material success. Even Sandy Koufax was criticized for his decision to sit out a World Series game against the Minnesota Twins that took place on Yom Kippur, as sports columnist Don Riley quipped, "And the Twins love matzah balls on Thursdays." But these forces are not only external. Often the battle between conflicting demands of the material and spiritual realms takes place within us. The High Holy Day process of introspection and *t'shuvah* can be instrumental in helping us balance our lives by helping us set and reset our priorities.

GLEANINGS

Another Version

Rabbi Chiya said: Terach was a manufacturer of idols. He once went away somewhere and left Abraham to sell them in his place. A man came and wished to buy one. "How old are you?" Abraham asked him.

"Fifty years," was the reply.

"Woe to such a man!" he exclaimed, "You are fifty years old and would worship a day-old object!"

At this he became ashamed and departed.

B'reishit Rabbah 33:13

They Cannot Hear

Their idols are but silver and gold,
the work of human hands.
They have a mouth, but they cannot speak;
they have eyes, but they cannot see;
they have ears, but they cannot hear;
they have a nose, but they cannot smell;
they have hands, but they cannot feel;
they have feet, but they cannot walk;
nor can they make a sound with their throat.
Those who make them

shall become like them,
whoever trusts in them.
O Israel, trust in the Eternal!
He is your help and your shield.

Psalm 115:4–9

Idolatry Today?

From Judaism's perspective, idolatry occurs when one holds any value (for instance, nationalism) higher than God. Thus, a person who, on the basis of "my country right or wrong," performs acts that God designates as wrong is an idolater; his behavior makes it clear that he regards his country's demand to do evil as more binding than God's demand to do good. Such a person's claim to worship God— an assertion that was actually made by some S.S. officers who worked in concentration camps— is plainly false; the person is an idolater, not a follower of God.

Joseph Telushkin, Biblical Literacy
(New York: William Morrow, 1977), page 425

Mitzvot as Idols

Said the Kotzker [Rebbe]: The prohibition against the making of idols includes within itself the prohibition against making idols out of the [mitzvot]. One should never imagine that the chief purpose of a [mitzvah] is its outward form [i.e., the doing], and that its inward meaning should be subordinated [i.e., the devotion with which it is done].

Cited in The Chasidic Anthology, ed. Louis I. Newman
(New York: Schocken Books, 1963), page 193

God Dethroned

When God is dethroned, His throne does not remain empty for long. Some false god, some Wotan, Moloch, Mammon, or Mars soon occupies it.

A. H. Silver, World Crisis 1941, page 80; cited in A Treasury
of Jewish Quotations, ed. Joseph L. Baron (Northvale,
N.J.: Jason Aronson Inc., 1985), page 195

Spiritual Reality

Either there is God who is the creative energy of the universe, or there is not. Those are our only two choices. God made us, or we made up God. Place your bets and live accordingly. We can do this consciously or unconsciously, but do it we must. Most people, even while saying they do believe, live as if there is no God. They have replaced God with an ideology, a state, a cause, or themselves. They become the sole determinant in how they live their lives. And so they live without awe, without wonder, without a will greater than their own. And this is death.

Terry Bookman, The Busy Soul (New York: Perigree, 1999),
page 131

To Praise God

Built into the notion of Creation are limits and boundaries, and the rest of creation knows and respects their place. But people who are less aware that all being interconnects bump up against the limits and are less likely to praise the name of the Lord. To praise God is to be, and to be what you are most fully.

Carol Ochs, Song of the Self (Valley Forge, Pa.:
Trinity Press International, 1994), page 73

Adam Made Mortal

R. Chama ben R. Chanina said: Adam deserved to be spared the experience of death. Why then was the penalty of death decreed against him? Because the Holy One, blessed be He, foresaw that Nebuchadnezzar and Hiram would declare themselves gods; therefore was death decreed against him.

B'reishit Rabbah 9:5

Israel's Humility

The Holy One, blessed be He, said to Israel: "I desire you, for even when I confer greatness upon you, you humble yourselves before Me; but the idol worshipers are not like this. I conferred greatness upon Nimrod, and he said: 'Come, let us build a city for ourselves [Genesis 11:4].'"

Babylonian Talmud, Chulin 89a

The Love of God

How can we discover the love of God within us, if, instead of using every possible means to become imbued with such love, we make no effort whatever to cultivate it? Whence shall come to us the ecstatic communion with God and His Torah, if we give no thought to the greatness of God? For without comprehending God's greatness it is impossible to enter into communion with Him.

Moses Chayyim Luzzato, *Mesillat Yesharim*, trans. Mordecai M. Kaplan (Philadelphia: Jewish Publication Society, 1948), page 5

Love is a Verb

How do you love people? You do selfless things for them. You do things which don't necessarily benefit you. Sometimes they don't benefit you in any way at all. In this sense, every favor can be the beginning of love or at least its repair. Each favor is a gift of self that says, "You mean more to me than me. I may not understand your motive; it is enough for me to know that you desire it."

This is also the idea behind religious deeds. We cannot comprehend why God wants what God wants. Indeed, the more incomprehensible, the more likely we do them solely in response to the divine and not for some baser, ulterior, secret, personal motive. Besides, if they made perfect sense, we'd do them ourselves, without being asked.

Lawrence Kushner, *The Book of Words* (Woodstock, Vt.: Jewish Lights, 1993), pp. 71–72

With All Your Heart

What is the appropriate love for God? It is to love God with a great and exceeding love, a love so strong that one's soul is bound with the love of God. One should daily contemplate upon it, like someone who is lovesick, whose mind is never free from his passion for someone. For he thinks of her at all times, when sitting down and when rising up, eating or drinking. The love of God should be even more intense. One should contemplate upon it always, as God has commanded, "with all your heart and with all your soul" (Deuteronomy 6:5).

Maimonides, *Mishneh Torah*, "Laws of Penitence," 10:3

Penitence Out of Love

Every thought of penitence joins all the past to the future, thereby is the future exalted in the ascent of the will motivated by penitence out of love.

Avraham Yitzchak Kook, *The Lights of Penitence*, 7:2, trans. A. B. Z. Metzger (New York: Yeshiva University Press, 1968), page 45

Never Too Late

After some time Elisha ben Avuyah (the former Sage and current heretic, also known as "Acher") was taken ill, and they came and told Rabbi Meir, "Elisha your master is sick." He went to him and appealed to him, "Return in penitence." He said to him, "Will they accept me after all this?" He responded, "Is it not written, 'You turn a human being to contrition' [Psalm 90:3], even when one's life is crushed." At that, Elisha ben Avuyah burst into tears and died. And Rabbi Meir rejoiced and said, "It appears that my master passed away in the midst of repentance."

Ruth Rabbah 6:4

Jonah in Nineveh

On the third occasion God sent him against Nineveh to destroy it, Jonah argued with himself, saying, "I know that the nations are near to repentance; now they will repent and the Holy One, blessed be He, will direct His anger against Israel. And is it not enough for me that Israel should call me a lying prophet; but shall also the nations of the world do likewise? Therefore, behold, I will escape from His presence to a place where His glory is not declared."

Pirkei D'Rabbi Eliezer, chapter 10

Bringing Near

"And Abram took Sarai his wife, and Lot their brother's son, and all their possessions that they had gathered, and the souls that they had made in Haran" [Genesis 12:5].

Rabbi Elazar observed in the name of Rabbi Yosei ben Zimra: If all the nations assembled to create one insect, they could not endow it with life, yet you say, "And the souls that they had made!" It refers, however, to the converts (that they had made). Then let them say, "That they had converted"; why "That they had made"? That is to teach you that he who brings a worshiper of stars [idolater] near [to God] is as though he created him.

B'reishit Rabbah 39:14

Admonition

It is related of Rabbi Heshel (18th–19th cent.) that he had an admonisher who stood watch over him even during his sermon, and when he would recognize anything at all unseemly in any sentiment of Rabbi Heshel's, he would admonish him in the presence of the entire congregation. Rabbi Heshel would accept the admonition and stop in the middle of his sermon.

N. Harari, cited by S. Y. Agnon, *Days of Awe* (New York: Schocken Books, 1965) page 135

Isaac

Early in the morning the sun took a walk in the forest
Together with me and with Father
And my right hand in his left.

Like lightning a knife flamed between the trees.
And I fear so the terror of my eyes facing blood on the leaves.

Father, Father hurry and save Isaac
And no one will be missing at lunchtime.

It is I who am being slaughtered, my son,
And my blood is already on the leaves.
And Father's voice was stifled.
And his face pale.

And I wanted to cry out, wishing not to believe,
And tearing open the eyes.
And I woke up.

And helpless-of-blood was the right hand.

A. Gilboa, "Isaac," in *The Modern Hebrew Poem Itself*, ed. Stanley Brunshaw, T. Carmi, and Ezra Spicehandler (Cambridge, Mass.: Harvard University Press, 1989), page 136

A Foyer of T'shuvah

Rabbi Yaakov said, "This world is like a foyer before the world-to-come. Prepare yourself in the foyer so that you will be able to enter the banquet hall."

He would often say, "An hour spent in penitence and good deeds in this world is better than all of life in the world-to-come. An hour of contentment in the world-to-come is better than all of life in this world."

Pirkei Avot 4:16, 17

The Sh'ma: Witness to Oneness

The six words of the *Sh'ma*—Deuteronomy 6:4, שְׁמַע יִשְׂרָאֵל יי אֱלֹהֵינוּ יי אֶחָד (*Sh'ma Yisrael Adonai Eloheinu Adonai Echad*), "Hear, O Israel: the Eternal is our God, the Eternal is One"—hold an unparalleled position of importance in Jewish practice, according to Rabbi Gunther Plaut. Historically, in keeping with the example of Rabbi Akiva (as reported in Babylonian Talmud *B'rachot* 61b), these words have been uttered by countless Jewish martyrs at the moment of their passing. Liturgically, this verse has become the best-known phrase of our prayer service, one of its most ancient rubrics, the "watchword" of our faith, the witness to the Divine Unity. Traditionally, the *Sh'ma* is recited in both morning and evening services and before retiring at night, and it is inextricably tied to the Days of Awe as evidenced by its threefold repetition at the end of the *N'ilah* service. It is this phrase, followed immediately by

"The Eternal One is God" (from I Kings 18:39) and one long shofar blast that virtually conclude the High Holy Day period.

That God is One, as articulated in the *Sh'ma,* can be considered the most fundamental principle of monotheism. This declaration is seen as the major concept that differentiates the Jewish worldview from that of pagan society. Rabbi Y'hudah HaNasi (Judah the Prince) thought the responsibility of reciting the *Sh'ma* to be so essential that he chose to begin the Mishnah with its explanation. According to the Talmud, the recitation of the *Sh'ma* is known as קַבָּלַת עוֹל מַלְכוּת שָׁמַיִם (*kabbalat ol malchut shamayim*), "the acceptance of the yoke of the rulership of heaven," implying that through verbal statement, worshipers declare, accept, and come to understand their commitment to God's role in their lives. In fact, the very word, שְׁמַע (*sh'ma*), can not only mean to hear, in the simple auditory sense, but can also indicate one's responsibility to actively "understand" and "accept."

The importance of this concept is emphasized by the scribal convention of the Torah scroll. The Masoretic tradition provides for the *ayin* (ע) of the first word (שְׁמַע, *sh'ma*) to be enlarged. Similarly, the final *dalet* (ד) of the last word (אֶחָד, *echad*) appears enlarged. *Sefer Rokeach* explains that together these two enlarged letters spell *eid* (עֵד), the Hebrew term for "witness." Whenever we proclaim the *Sh'ma,* we bear testimony to God's existence, efficaciousness, and unity. Thus, the prophet Isaiah, in reminding Israel of God's uniqueness as Creator, as well as the Divine's redemptive role in history, reports in God's name, "You are my witnesses" (Isaiah 43:10).

Maimonides' Laws of T'shuvah

Maimonides, also known as Rabbi Moshe ben Maimon or, more commonly, by the acronym Rambam, was a twelfth-century scholar who was born in Spain and lived most of his days in Egypt. Maimonides wrote extensively on Jewish law and philosophy.

In his famous code of Jewish law, the *Mishneh Torah,* or "Repetition of the Torah," Maimonides includes ten chapters dedicated to the laws of *t'shuvah,* which he indicates is a positive commandment. That is, *t'shuvah* appears as one of the 248 prescriptions to do something (as opposed to the 365 prohibitions found in the Torah). Essential to Maimonides' approach is *cheshbon hanefesh,* the self-examination that leads to the awareness of having missed the mark. Once we are cognizant of our shortcomings, the Rambam deems it essential that we confess verbally before God. That is, we appear before God acknowledging our wrongdoings, expressing regret, and promising never to do it again: "Please, God, I have missed the mark, I have sinned, I have transgressed before You in that I have done such and such. And behold, I am sorry, I am ashamed by what I have done. And never will I again do this."

Maimonides emphasizes that the above confession must not be empty lip service. Rather, these words and their intentions must be taken completely to heart. But more than that, the Rambam stresses that true repentance involves action (or in some cases of temptation, the lack of it). "What constitutes complete repentance? When one is confronted by the identical situation wherein he sinned, and it is within his power to sin again. However, he abstains! He does not do it on account of *t'shuvah,* and not because of fear or lack of strength" (*Mishneh Torah,* "Laws of Penitence," 2:1; paraphrasing Babylonian Talmud, *Yoma* 86b).

In his *Tales of the Chasidim,* Martin Buber relates a tale that typifies the Maimonidean approach to repentance with its focus upon behavior: Rabbi Simcha Bunam of Pzsha once asked his disciples, "How can we tell when a sin we have committed has been pardoned?"

His disciples offered various answers, but none of them pleased the rabbi. "We can tell," he answered, "by the fact that we no longer commit that sin."

Chapter 5

What It Means to Be God's Servant: Idol Smashing

When the king learns that the masses are turning to the God of Abraham, his heart becomes saddened. His counselors again advise him, as they have done in the past, to call for a major seven-day, religious festival. The people shall don their fancy embroidery, precious stones, and amulets made of gold and silver, and they shall eat and drink in their idolatrous gardens and meeting places. When Abraham sees the physical wealth of the people, they tell Nimrod, he will be so swayed that he will "reenter" the king's faith, though he had never actually been part of it.

The king declares the idolatrous holiday and orders Terach, Abraham's father, to bring his son to witness the vast riches of his kingdom. Abraham claims to be unable to go. Terach agrees to leave without Abraham to celebrate with his god, the king, on the proviso that his son watch over his and the king's idols while he's away.

Alone with the idols, Abraham takes an axe and smashes them, with the exception of the largest, in whose hand he places the axe. Upon conclusion of the idolatrous festival, Nimrod returns to see his smashed idols. When the king demands to know what has happened, Abraham tells him that the large idol became angry at the others and smashed them with the axe he still grasps in his hand. Nimrod becomes enraged and orders Abraham to be imprisoned without the benefit of food or drink.

Probably the most familiar of midrashic metaphors concerning the early life of Abraham, the smashing of the idols signifies not only the Patriarch's iconoclastic role in the external world, but perhaps his inner struggles as well. All of us are prone, as were the king and his counselors, to making the same mistakes over and over again. Everyone of us is liable to delude ourselves now and again. There comes a point, however, when, if we are to move forward in our lives, we must honestly confront those inner demons, those internal idols, those false assumptions that prevent us from becoming the people we are meant to be. The weight of these idols must be smashed before we can take the desired positive step up.

The High Holy Days afford us the opportunity to take that step. When we set aside these Days of Awe to examine our ways, to take accounting of those idols we still harbor in our hearts, and to eradicate them, we are able to achieve that higher image of ourselves to which we aspire.

Whereas in the previous chapter Abraham was called upon to promote idolatry (through participation in the family business), this chapter challenges the Patriarch with the imperative to merely guard the images, the idolatrous traditions of his family and his society. As usual, Abraham responds not by passively looking the other way, but through swift and courageous action as God's servant.

5:1	During the feast, the king told Terach, the father of Abraham,	וַיְהִי בְּתוֹךְ יְמֵי הַמִּשְׁתֶּה וַיֹּאמֶר הַמֶּלֶךְ לְתֶרַח אֲבִי אַבְרָהָם
5:3	to bring his son, Abraham, to see the greatness and vast riches and	לְהָבִיא אֶת בְּנוֹ לִרְאוֹת גְּדוּלָתוֹ וְעוֹשֶׁר,
5:5	glory of his kingdom, and the multitude of his ministers	כְּבוֹד מַלְכוּתוֹ, וְרוֹב שָׂרָיו
5:7	and his servants. Terach said to his son, "My son, Abraham! Come with me	וַעֲבָדָיו. וַיֹּאמֶר תֶּרַח לִבְנוֹ, "בְּנִי אַבְרָהָם בֹּא עִמִּי
5:9	to the festival of the king, Nimrod, our god."	לְמוֹעֵד הַמֶּלֶךְ נִמְרוֹד אֱלֹהֵינוּ."
5:11	Abraham said, "I am not able to go there."	אָמַר אַבְרָהָם, "אֵינִי יָכוֹל לָצֵאת לְשָׁם."
5:13	Terach said to him, "If that is so, you stay with the idols until	אָמַר לוֹ תֶּרַח, "אִם כֵּן בְּנִי תֵשֵׁב עִם הַצְּלָמִים עַד
5:15	we return." And he did so. So, Terach went.	בּוֹאֵנוּ מִשָּׁם." וַיַּעַשׂ כֵּן וַיֵּלֶךְ תֶּרַח.
5:17	And Abraham remained with the idols. And	וַיֵּשֶׁב אַבְרָהָם עִם הַצְּלָמִים, וְגַם
5:19	the king's idols were also there.	צַלְמֵי הַמֶּלֶךְ הָיוּ שָׁם.

P'shat: 5:8. My son. Terach appeals to Abraham as a member of the family, his son. **5:10. our god.** Again the term "our" subtly points to the family and national tradition. **5:19. king's idols.** These may be idols owned by the king and/or those fashioned in Nimrod's image.

D'rash: 5:8. My son. This echoes the story of the Binding of Isaac (chapter 22 of the Book of Genesis), in which the phrase "my son" appears as a *leitvort* connoting the relationship between father and son and the great pathos of the situation. **5:9. festival.** The term מוֹעֵד *(mo-eid)*, translated here as "festival," is the same word used by the Torah to denote "an appointed time of the Eternal." That is, מוֹעֵד *(mo-eid)* points to one of the festivals of God and the Jewish people. **5:11–12. I am not able.** The Hebrew term for "able," יָכוֹל *(yachol)*, is

50

also used to imply God's omnipotence. Abraham's statement, therefore, rings as a satirical aside emphasizing God's uniqueness: "While Nimrod may pretend to be 'able' or omnipotent, I [Abraham], knowing my place as a human being, am most assuredly not." Understanding our limitations is as critical for us as it was for Abraham. For part of this High Holy Day process of renewal involves forgiveness, not only of others, but of our imperfect selves. **5:14–15. you stay…until we return**. This again parallels the *Akeidah*, where Abraham says to his servants, "'Stay here with the donkey, and I and the lad will go there, and we will worship, and return to you'" (Genesis 22:5). Just as the *Akeidah* is regarded as a supreme test of Abraham's faith—in the words of *B'reishit Rabbah*, "held high as an ensign" for all to see—so may this situation be regarded as a trial for the young Abraham that serves to edify and inspire all who learn of it.

5:20 When Abraham saw that	וַיַּרְא אַבְרָהָם כִּי
the king went to his meeting	הָלַךְ הַמֶּלֶךְ אֶל בֵּית
5:22 place, he took an axe in his hand,	הוֹעֵד אֲשֶׁר לוֹ וַיִּקַּח בְּיָדוֹ גַּרְזֶן
and as he saw the idols of the	וְכִרְאוֹתוֹ צַלְמֵי
5:24 king sitting, he said,	הַמֶּלֶךְ יוֹשְׁבִים אָמַר,
"The Eternal, He is God,"	"יי הוּא הָאֱלֹהִים,"
5:26 and he pushed them off their thrones	וַיַּשְׁלִיכֵם מֵעַל כִּסְאָם
to the ground, and he smote	אַרְצָה וַיַּךְ בָּהֶם מַכָּה
5:28 them mightily. With the large	רַבָּה וּגְדוֹלָה. בַּגָּדוֹל
ones he began, and with the	הֵחֵל,
5:30 small ones he finished.	וּבַקָּטָן כָּלָה.
He lopped off this one's hands,	לָזֶה קָטַע יָדָיו,
5:32 he cut off this one's head and	לָזֶה כָּרַת רֹאשׁוֹ,
blinded this one's eyes,	וְלָזֶה שָׁבַר עֵינָיו,
5:34 he broke that one's legs,	וְלָזֶה שָׁבַר אֶת רַגְלָיו.
and when all of them were broken,	וְכֻלָּם נִשְׁבָּרִים,
5:36 Abraham went out.	וַיֵּצֵא אַבְרָהָם.

P'shat: **5:21. the king went**. The information indicates that Abraham smashes the idols at the same moment that the king is leading the idolatrous frenzy in his temple, making the contrast even starker. **5:25. The Eternal, He is God**. Abraham acts out of religious conviction, not personal sentiment. **5:28–30. large ones he began…small ones he finished**. This merism indicates the fullness of the rout. **5:35. all of them were broken**. With the exception of the very largest idol.

D'rash: 5:21–22. meeting place. The term בֵּית הַוֹעֵד (beit ho-eid) may also refer to a temple. Its appearance here, therefore, parallels the frequent use of אֹהֶל מוֹעֵד (ohel mo-eid) by the Torah to indicate the Israelites' portable Sanctuary in the wilderness. **5:28–29. With the large ones he began.** Contrary to the popular opinion, as expressed by the old woman in chapter 4, size is no indicator of an idol's power. In fact, large and small alike fall victim to Abraham's axe. **5:36. Abraham went out.** In Mishnaic Hebrew, the term "went out" refers to fulfilling one's obligation to God. For instance, *Mishnah B'rachot* (2:1) relates: "If one was studying the Torah and the time for the recitation of the *Sh'ma* arrived, if one directed his mind [to fulfill the mitzvah of reciting the *Sh'ma*], יָצָא [yatza]." He, literally, "went out of" his obligation; he has fulfilled his duty to God. Abraham thus refuses to accompany his father to celebrate the king's holiday, for by doing so he would be "unable to go out," that is, unable to fulfill his obligation to God. By destroying the idols, however, the Patriarch does fulfill his religious duty and destiny.

5:37 When the days of the feast were completed, the king returned home.	וַיִּשְׁלְמוּ יְמֵי הַמִּשְׁתֶּה וַיָּבֹא הַמֶּלֶךְ אֶל בֵּיתוֹ.
5:39 But, before this, when he was smashing them, he put the axe	וְקוֹדֶם זֶה כְּשֶׁשִּׁבֵּר אוֹתָם שָׁם הַגַּרְזֶן
5:41 in the hand of the largest of the idols. When the king saw his idols were	בְּיַד גְּדוֹל הַצְּלָמִים. וּכְרְאוֹת הַמֶּלֶךְ אֶת צְלָמָיו
5:43 smashed, he said, "Who was here? And who is it that has filled his heart	שְׁבוּרִים, אָמַר, "מִי הָיָה כָאן? וּמִי הוּא אֲשֶׁר מִלְאוֹ לִבּוֹ
5:45 to do thusly?" And all the people answered, crying,	לַעֲשׂוֹת כֵּן?" וַיַּעֲנוּ כָּל הָעָם בּוֹכִים
5:47 and they said, "Our lord the king, you should know that Abraham stayed	וְאָמְרוּ, "אֲדוֹנֵינוּ הַמֶּלֶךְ תֵּדַע שֶׁאַבְרָהָם הָיָה יוֹשֵׁב
5:49 with them. We heard that he was breaking them."	אֶצְלָם. וְשָׁמַעְנוּ שֶׁהָיָה מְשַׁבֵּר לָהֶם".
5:51 The king commanded that Abraham be brought before him.	וַיְצַו הַמֶּלֶךְ לְהָבִיא אֶת אַבְרָהָם לְפָנָיו.
5:53 And they brought him. The king and his ministers said to him,	וַיְבִיאוּ אוֹתוֹ. וַיֹּאמְרוּ לוֹ הַמֶּלֶךְ וְשָׂרָיו,
5:55 "Why did you shatter our gods?"	"לָמָה שִׁבַּרְתָּ אֶת אֱלֹהֵינוּ?"

P'shat: 5:39. when he was smashing them. That is, when Abraham was smashing the idols. **5:49. We heard.** Whether "all the people" who are speaking to the king actually heard the idols being smashed or whether they inform the king on the basis of hearsay is unclear.

D'rash: **5:39. when he was smashing them**. Many versions of Abraham's destruction of the idols exist. This legend of Abraham smashing the idols is so well known that *Midrash D'Avraham Avinu,* a minor medieval midrashic text that presents the story of Abraham's early life, begins with a confrontation between Abraham and Nimrod concerning the idol-smashing incident, which the author obviously assumes the reader to already know. **5:49. We heard**. This echoes Daniel 3:8–12 in which a group of "certain Chaldeans" inform the king of "certain Jews," Shadrach, Meshach, and Abed-Nego, who have not complied with the royal decree concerning mandatory idol worship. A similar parallel is found in Esther 3:8, which depicts Haman's bid to the king for permission to murder all the Jews: "There is a certain people . . . their laws are different from every other people's. They do not observe the king's laws, therefore it is not befitting the king to tolerate them." These statements, of course, all point to our minority status as Jews and the reality that not all of our neighbors admire or even approve of our Jewishness. This is especially true when our behaviors are regarded as iconoclastic, challenging popularly held assumptions and values. **5:55. Why did you shatter**. This again parallels the scene in the Book of Daniel (3:13–14) in which King Nebuchadnezzar, amidst his rage, has Shadrach, Meshach, and Abed-Nego brought before him. He then questions them whether it is true that they failed to worship his idol. These occurrences highlight the fact that living as a Jew requires the fortitude to be different.

5:56	He said to them, "I didn't	וַיֹּאמֶר לָהֶם, "אֲנִי לֹא
	break them, no. Rather, the large	שָׁבַרְתִּי אוֹתָם, לֹא. כִּי אִם הַגָּדוֹל
5:58	one of them smashed them.	שֶׁבָּהֶם שִׁבֵּר אוֹתָם.
	Don't you see that the axe is in	הֲלֹא תִרְאֶה הֱיוֹת הַגַּרְזֶן
5:60	his hand? And if you won't	בְּיָדוֹ? וְאִם לֹא
	believe it, ask him and he will	תַּאֲמִין בִּי תִּשְׁאַל מִמֶּנּוּ וְהוּא
5:62	tell."	יַגִּיד."
	And as he heard his words,	וְכִשְׁמָעוֹ דְבָרָיו
5:64	he became angry to the point of	חָרָה לוֹ עַד
	killing him. And he said to	מָוֶת וַיֹּאמֶר
5:66	imprison him.	לְהוֹלִיכוֹ לְבֵית הַסּוֹהַר.
	He commanded the prison warden	וַיְצַו אֶל שַׂר בֵּית הַסּוֹהַר
5:68	to refrain from giving him bread to eat	לְבִלְתִּי תֵת לוֹ פַּת לֶאֱכֹל
	or water to drink.	וְלֹא מַיִם לִשְׁתּוֹת.

P'shat: **5:61–62. ask him and he will tell**. Abraham again appeals to logic as a means of dispelling the scourge of idolatry. **5:63. he heard his words**. Nimrod hears Abraham's explanation of what happened to the idols. **5:65–66. he said to imprison him**. Nimrod orders Abraham to be incarcerated for the heresy of breaking the images.

D'rash: **5:66. imprison him.** *Pirkei D'Rabbi Eliezer* lists Abraham's imprisonment as one of his ten trials. **5:68–69. bread to eat or water to drink.** This parallels the story of Joseph, whose brothers cast him into an empty pit, "in which there is no water" (Genesis 37:24). Joseph's being cast into the pit is regarded as part of a chain of events that leads to the Jewish people's descending into Egypt, becoming enslaved there, and emerging to accept God's mission as a "kingdom of priests and a holy nation" (Exodus 19:6). So, too, may Abraham's incarceration be seen as one occurrence in a chain of events establishing the Patriarch as the first Jew, bringing knowledge of the One God and of the divine demand for loving, ethical behavior to the forefront of humanity.

GLEANINGS

Set Bread and Water

He [Abraham] set bread and water before all the people of the world, and he led them to righteousness by speaking persuasively. "Whom do you serve?" he would ask them. "Serve the Eternal, the God of heaven and earth." And he would expound to them until they repented. Even the guilty he led to righteousness.

Zohar 1:264b

Hitting the Idols

In his father's house they worshiped idols. They used to make graven images and give them to Abraham to sell in the market. When a person would come to buy a graven image from him, Abraham would take a mallet and bang each idol, asking, "Do you want this one or that one?" Upon seeing him hit the idols, the customer would immediately go away.

Midrash HaGadol, B'reishit 12:1

Destroying Idols

A Jew is one who opposes every sort of idolatry.

Babylonian Talmud, *M'gillah* 13a

Power within God

...The power lies within God, not in our conception of God nor within the image we make for God.

Obviously, there aren't a lot of clay figurine worshipers anymore; but that doesn't mean we lack idols. It's just that our idols have different shapes these days. Money is one of those. When we commit unethical acts for the sake of money, we are committing idolatry. When we use money to keep the poor powerless, we are committing idolatry. When we live to make money instead of making money to live, we are committing idolatry. Because in all these cases, money has become the highest power.

Mark S. Bloom, *Out of the Mouths of Babes* (1998), pages 16–17

Gardens and Delights

Those who serve God from love will be like servants who lay out gardens and delights with which to please their absent lord when he returns.

Tanna D'Vei Eliyahu, 560

Inner Process to Iconoclasm

The inner process of search ("roaming his mind"), is accompanied by physical expressions of rejection, anger, a kind of impatience approaching contempt for the unenlightened responses of his world and indeed of himself— "How long shall we bow down?..." The anger of his iconoclasm is literally enacted here in the smashing of idols....

Avivah Gottlieb Zornberg, *The Beginning of Desire: Reflections on Genesis* (New York: Image Books, 1995), page 84

Distancing Himself

Until Abraham could distance himself from what had defined him as an adolescent—the culture, mythology, and mores of the society in which he was raised, and his family's customs and stories—he could not begin to search for his real self. He had begun to recognize that he existed separately from the surroundings of his youth. In turn, this realization propelled him toward his ultimate destiny.

Norman Cohen, *Voices from Genesis: Guiding Us through the Stages of Life* (Woodstock, Vt.: Jewish Lights, 1998), page 72

Transcendent Spiritual Identity

We are entitled to enjoy the fruits of our labor, and the material plane provides many of the blessings of life on earth. The problem arises when we define ourselves and our sense of self-worth by lifeless objects—as our consumer society constantly encourages us to do. And while we may achieve a short-term sense of security by driving the "right" car or wearing this season's fashions, they will not sustain us through inevitable periods of loneliness, sadness, and pain. Only by believing in our transcendent identity with God do we achieve an enduring sense of self-worth that is immune to the vicissitudes of life.

Naomi H. Rosenblatt and Joshua Horwitz, *Wrestling with Angels* (New York: Delta, 1995), page 84

The Seven Noachide Laws

The great medieval scholar Rabbi Shlomo Yitzchaki (commonly known by the acronym Rashi), in his commentary upon the *Sh'ma*, discerns the sweep of history: "Hear, O Israel: the Eternal is our God," today; eventually, "the Eternal will be One." This idea is similarly represented by the traditional version of the *Aleinu* prayer in the "Sovereignty" (*Malchuyot*) section of the Rosh HaShanah liturgy. The prayer begins with "our" obligation toward God and progresses to the day when "God will be One, and God's name will be One." Most scholars agree, however, that this does not mean that all peoples will eventually be converted to Judaism. Rather, the day when "the Eternal will be One" is a vision of an era when all humanity will as one accept and live by God's basic moral code for all peoples, the Seven Noachide Laws.

While the Rabbis read the Torah as obligating the Jewish people to a total of 613 commandments, they see the "Seven Laws of the Children of Noah" as the heritage of all peoples, having been established in the covenant between God and Noah after the Flood. Although differences of opinion exist as to the nuances of the seven universal ethical prescriptions, there is agreement that all the precepts may be viewed as essential to the maintenance of a decent society. The Seven Noachide Laws are (1) prohibition against idolatry, (2) not blaspheming God, (3) the establishment of courts of justice, (4) not spilling blood needlessly, (5) not committing adultery, (6) not robbing, and (7) not eating flesh from a living animal.

Abraham's greatness lay in his ability to spread God's universal code of morality, the Seven Noachide Laws, among all the families of the earth. His willingness to break down the barriers to the achievement of his goal, his smashing the prohibited idols, attests not only to his methodology, but to his courage.

For us, Abraham's iconoclasm points to the fact that it is not enough to merely serve as an example of goodness. Sometimes it is necessary to fight actively to eradicate evil. For it is only by tearing down the walls of evil that distance the world from righteous behavior that the dream of universal morality will ever be achieved.

The Chasidic master the S'fat Emet, in his commentary to *Pirkei Avot,* points out that this iconoclastic process can also be an internal one. He sees Abraham's efforts as a determination to raise himself spiritually in order to achieve his divine destiny. To accomplish this, Abraham had to smash the idols within. He had to break through those internal impediments to his personal growth.

The High Holy Day process of *cheshbon hanefesh* (soul searching) is a call to find and eradicate the idols within. In this way, we are able to raise ourselves spiritually and ethically to the point at which we can be effective in promoting the observance of God's universal morality (the Seven Noachide Laws) to all the families of the earth and live out our sacred mission as a light to the nations.

Chapter 6

The Efficacy of Prayer and Good Intentions: The Fiery Furnace

While in prison, the Patriarch demonstrates the efficacy of prayer and good intentions as he prays to God to save him. In a show of divine mercy, the Holy One causes a fountain to appear for Abraham in the prison and sends the angel Gabriel to stay with Abraham and provide food throughout the year of his imprisonment. Since Gabriel also suckled Abraham as a baby, his reappearance here speaks to the human need for God's nurturing at all stages of life. Judaism can be a source of strength to us in childhood, in adulthood, and throughout our lives.

As Abraham sits in prison, Nimrod seeks a "final solution" to his Abraham (and God) problem. Upon the advice of his court, the king builds a fiery furnace so that he may immolate Abraham and uproot faith in God. When those who attempt to hurl Abraham into the fire are themselves burned, Nimrod accepts Satan's counsel and builds a catapult. They bind Abraham and place him in the catapult. Satan, Abraham's mother, and the king all entice the Patriarch to save himself by bowing down to Nimrod. But Abraham's faith in God remains strong. God, perceiving the sincerity of his devotion, personally effects redemption for Abraham and all those around him.

This chapter presents the ultimate challenge of this midrash. The fiery furnace symbolizes the idolatrous world's most severe threats of physical annihilation and spiritual death. Abraham's visitors—Satan, his mother, and the king—represent the temptations and pressures that militate against the leading of a righteous life. Through his connection with God, Abraham proves that not only is it possible to emerge from the furnace alive, but faith and righteousness can change one's life and the entire world for the better.

On another level, the fiery furnace is the power that the High Holy Days have to confront us with our mortality. *Maaseh Avraham Avinu* teaches that it is possible to come away from the Days of Awe, and in particular Yom Kippur, not only physically intact, but spiritually cleansed. Our relationship with God, efforts at *t'shuvah,* and the behaviors that emerge from this period bear the power to transform our lives in significant ways.

The chapter begins with Abraham bound in the catapult about to be hurled into the fire. It concludes with Abraham sitting among the angels, in a garden where the furnace had once been, amidst the affirmations of the formerly idolatrous people, crying, "The Eternal, He is God!"

6:1	They took Abraham	וַיִּקְחוּ אֶת אַבְרָהָם
	and tied his arms, hands, and legs	וַיִּקְשְׁרוּ זְרוֹעָיו, יָדָיו, וְרַגְלָיו,
6:3	with a strong knot, and placed him in	בְּקֶשֶׁר חָזָק וַיָּשִׂימוּ אוֹתוֹ
	the *taraboku* to hurl him. But,	בַּטַּרַאבּוֹקוּ לְהַשְׁלִיכוֹ. וּכְרְאוֹת
6:5	when Abraham, our Patriarch,	אַבְרָהָם אָבִינוּ,
	of blessed memory, saw how they	עָלָיו הַשָּׁלוֹם, אֵיךְ
6:7	tied him, he raised his eyes to	קָשְׁרוּ אוֹתוֹ נָשָׂא עֵינָיו
	heaven and said, "Eternal, my	לְשָׁמַיִם וְאָמַר, "יי
6:9	God, You see what this evil one is	אֱלֹהַי אַתָּה רוֹאֶה אֶת אֲשֶׁר הוּא
	doing to me."	עוֹשֶׂה בִּי הָרָשָׁע הַזֶּה."
6:11	Also the angels on high	גַּם מַלְאֲכֵי מַעֲלָה
	said before the Holy One,	אָמְרוּ לִפְנֵי הַקָּדוֹשׁ
6:13	blessed be He, "Master of the	בָּרוּךְ הוּא, "רִבּוֹנוֹ שֶׁל
	universe, all the world is filled with	עוֹלָם, מַלֵּא כָּל הָאָרֶץ
6:15	your glory, have you not seen	כְּבוֹדֶךָ הֲלֹא רָאִיתָ
	what King Nimrod,	מַה עָשָׂה הַמֶּלֶךְ נִמְרוֹד
6:17	the blasphemer, has done to your	הַכּוֹפֵר
	servant and	בְּעַבְדְּךָ
6:19	your prophet, Abraham?"	וּנְבִיאֲךָ אַבְרָהָם?"

P'shat: **6:4. taraboku.** The technical term for the catapult. **6:4. hurl him.** Into the fiery furnace. **6:9. You see.** "Seeing" implies divine mercy.

D'rash: **6:2. tied his arms.** This echoes Genesis 22:9, which depicts Abraham binding his son Isaac and placing him upon the altar to be sacrificed. In performing the *Akeidah* (Binding of Isaac) then, Abraham is asking his son to go through what he himself has already experienced. (The same was the case of Abraham's behavior vis-à-vis the banishment of Hagar and Ishmael.) **6:4. taraboku.** The disparate spellings found among the various editions of the midrash indicate this to be a loan word. The building of the catapult points to God's uniqueness and God's might versus earthly (tyrannical) power. While God creates the world with all of the inherent ingredients for redemption (including a Torah to live by), Nimrod utilizes these bounties as well as the resources of intelligence and industry to devise technologies of death. **6:4. hurl.** The midrashic tradition of the fiery furnace is attested to in many sources. *Pirkei D'Rabbi Eliezer, Avot D'Rabbi Natan,* and the *Yalkut Shimoni* include the incident among Abraham's ten trials. *B'reishit Rabbah* 44:13 attests to Genesis 15:7 as the biblical source for the legend: "I am the Eternal who took you out of Ur of the Chaldees." Ur, the city of Abraham's birth, can also mean "fire." The "fire of the Chaldeans" then is identified with the fiery furnace in the midrash. **6:13–14. Master of the universe**. The angels on high are merely God's messengers. Though they dwell in the heights, even they do not fully comprehend God's essence and God's ways. There is but one Master of the universe. God's rulership over the whole of Creation is one of the major themes not only of this midrash, but of the Days of Awe.

6:20 The Holy One, blessed	אָמַר לָהֶם הַקָּדוֹשׁ בָּרוּךְ
be He, said to them, "How is it	הוּא, "אֵיךְ
6:22 possible not to know, when I	לֹא אֵדַע וְאָנֹכִי
know all the hidden things? But	יוֹדֵעַ כָּל הַנִּסְתָּרוֹת אֲבָל
6:24 I will show you vengeance	אֶרְאֶה אֲנִי לָכֶם נְקָמָה
upon Nimrod, the blasphemer,	בְּנִמְרוֹד הַכּוֹפֵר
6:26 and I will save Abraham,	וְאַצִּיל אֶת אַבְרָהָם
My servant."	עַבְדִּי."
6:28 The Maggid said that	אָמַר הַמַּגִּיד
Satan appeared to Abraham in	שֶׁהַשָּׂטָן בָּא אֵצֶל אַבְרָהָם
6:30 the likeness of a man and said	בִּדְמוּת אָדָם וְאָמַר
to him, "Abraham, if you want	לוֹ, "אַבְרָהָם אִם תִּרְצֶה
6:32 to save yourself from Nimrod's	לְהַצִּיל מֵאֵשׁ נִמְרוֹד
fire, prostrate yourself before	תִּשְׁתַּחֲוֶה אֵלָיו
6:34 him and believe in him."	וְהַאֲמֵן בּוֹ."

P'shat: **6:22–23. I know all**. One aspect of God's uniqueness is omniscience. **6:24. vengeance**. Revenge vis-à-vis God is understood as a "measure for measure" justice. That is, God metes out consequences prompted by and gauged to the particular sins of the individual. **6:33. prostrate yourself**. Prostration, again, is a sign of worship. **6:34. believe in him**. Satan suggests that Abraham publicly declare belief in Nimrod and denounce faith in God so that Abraham may save himself (despite the fact that the Patriarch will know the declaration to be false and dishonest).

D'rash: **6:29. Satan**. Rabbinic literature casts Satan as God's prosecuting attorney in the court on high. In this line of work, however, *HaSatan,* or "the Accuser," frequently appears a bit overzealous as he manifests (and represents) the tempting voice of human beings' baser thoughts and instincts. **6:33. prostrate yourself**. In Jewish tradition, prostration is only to be done before God. In the Book of Esther, Haman turns against Mordecai and the entire Jewish people because they refuse to bow down to him. **6:33–34. prostrate yourself... believe in him**. Satan's temptation of Abraham to abandon his highest principles in order to save himself parallels a story told in several rabbinic sources, including Babylonian Talmud

Gittin 57b and *Eichah Rabbah*. The tale concerns a woman (in some sources named Hannah) and her seven sons who are brought, one by one, before a king and told to bow down to an image. When the first six sons refuse, they are murdered. Finally, the last and youngest child is brought before the king. The king politely asks him to bow down to the idol. The boy refuses. The king asks him why. The boy quotes Deuteronomy 4:39, which is also included in the *Aleinu* prayer of our liturgy: "The Eternal One is God in the heavens above and the earth below; there is none else." The king tempts him, saying that his brothers experienced happiness in their lives, but he, at his tender age, has not yet. Therefore, if he bows down, the king promises to bestow favors upon him. But the young boy still refuses. The king again tempts him, offering to merely drop his ring and have the boy pick it up to lend the appearance of bowing down. But the boy, true to his God like Abraham, refuses. The boy is then martyred. Abraham is also willing to turn his life over for the "sanctification of God's name" (עַל קִדּוּשׁ הַשֵּׁם, *al kiddush HaShem*). For us, today, these stories of faith communicate that the attempt to live Jewishly and with integrity in our world, while not necessitating martyrdom, can often require deep devotion and sacrifice.

6:35	And as Abraham heard the words of Satan,	וַיְהִי כִּשְׁמוֹעַ אַבְרָהָם אֶת דִּבְרֵי הַשָּׂטָן,
6:37	he said to him, "May the Eternal rebuke you, Satan, inferior,	וַיֹּאמֶר לוֹ, "יִגְעַר יי בְּךָ הַשָּׂטָן, פָּחוּת,
6:39	contemptible, and accursed blasphemer!"	נִבְזֶה, אָרוּר כּוֹפֵר!"
6:41	He left him, and Abraham's mother came	וַיֵּצֵא מִלְּפָנָיו, וַתָּבֹא אִמּוֹ שֶׁל אַבְרָהָם
6:43	to kiss her son before they would throw him into the	לְנַשֵּׁק לִבְנָהּ קוֹדֶם שֶׁיַּשְׁלִיכוּ אוֹתוֹ לְתוֹךְ
6:45	fiery furnace. She said to him, "My son, bow down to	הַכִּבְשָׁן הָאֵשׁ. וַתֹּאמֶר לוֹ, "בְּנִי, תִּשְׁתַּחֲוֶה
6:47	Nimrod and convert to his faith, and you will be saved	לְנִמְרוֹד וְתִכָּנֵס תַּחַת אֱמוּנָתוֹ וְתִנָּצֵל
6:49	from the fiery furnace." Abraham said to her,	מִכִּבְשָׁן הָאֵשׁ." אָמַר לָהּ אַבְרָהָם,
6:51	"My mother, leave me!" and he pushed her from him.	"אִמִּי, תֵּלְכִי מֵעָלַי!" וְדָחַף אוֹתָהּ מֵעָלָיו.
6:53	And he said to her, "My mother, water can extinguish Nimrod's fire;	וַיֹּאמֶר לָהּ, "אִמִּי, אֵשׁ נִמְרוֹד תְּכַבֶּה אוֹתוֹ הַמַּיִם

6:55 but the fire of my God	אֲבָל אֵשׁ אֱלֹהַי
will never be extinguished, till	לָעַד לְעוֹלָם
6:57 the ends of time,	אֵינוֹ מְכוּבֶּה,
and [surely] water is not able to extinguish it."	וּמַיִם לֹא יוּכְלוּ לְכַבּוֹתוֹ".

P'shat: **6:37–38. May the Eternal rebuke you, Satan.** Abraham insists that the Accuser has become too zealous in his duty and that it will not work. Abraham will remain God's loyal servant, transcending the temptation to "sell out" in order to "save his skin." **6:41. He left him.** Rebuffed by Abraham's strong allegiance to God's truth, Satan exits the scene, defeated. **6:42–43. Abraham's mother came to kiss her son.** Abraham's mother represents the strong pull of family in all of our lives. **6:58. water is not able to extinguish it.** While Nimrod's fire remains subject to the laws of nature (water will extinguish it), God and His fire are entirely and uniquely above nature.

D'rash: **6:37–38. May the Eternal rebuke you, Satan.** This language echoes the prophetic vision of Zechariah (Zechariah 3:2) in which the Eternal rebukes Satan and describes the high priest at the time of the building of the Second Temple (Joshua) as "a brand plucked from the fire"—that is, something precious snatched from destruction, so that he may complete his mission of rebuilding the Temple and rekindling the menorah's light. The intimation here is one of Abraham's faith, that he too will be "plucked" from the fires of idolatry, immorality, and destruction, to complete his mission of spreading the light of God's morality and kindness around the world. **6:46–51. My son…My mother.** The repetition of these pronouns not only communicates the pathos of this situation, but again echoes the trial of the *Akeidah* (Binding of Isaac), which features the phrases "my son…my father." **6:55. the fire of my God.** Deuteronomy 33:2 describes the Torah as fire: "…at His right hand was a fiery law unto them." Significantly, *Pirkei D'Rabbi Eliezer* (chapter 26) states that God saved Abraham from the fire of Nimrod with His right hand. Since the right hand connotes strength, we can conclude that Torah is God's strength, which will not be extinguished. It is Torah, and our adherence to it, that are responsible for defeating the immoral Nimrods of the world and for the amazing survival of the Jewish people. Thus we read in Zechariah 4:6, "Not by might [the army], nor by power, but by My spirit, says the Eternal of Hosts."

6:59 And when his mother heard his	וּכְשֶׁשָּׁמְעָה אִמּוֹ דְּבָרָיו
words that they were true, she said	דִּבְרֵי צַדִּיקִים אָמְרָה
6:61 to him, "May the God whom you	לוֹ, "הָאֱלֹהִים אֲשֶׁר אַתָּה
serve, save you from the fire of	עוֹבֵד הוּא יַצִּילְךָ מֵאֵשׁ
6:63 Nimrod."	נִמְרוֹד".
And when they took Abraham and	וַיְהִי אַחֲרֵי כֵן וַיִּקְחוּ אֶת אַבְרָהָם

6:65	placed him in the launching pad of the catapult to throw him into the	וַיְשִׂימוּ בְּכַף הַטְּרַאבּוֹקוּ לְהַשְׁלִיךְ אוֹתוֹ
6:67	midst of the furnace, the ministering angels sought mercy from the Holy	לְתוֹךְ הַכִּבְשָׁן. וּמַלְאֲכֵי הַשָּׁרֵת בִּקְשׁוּ רַחֲמִים מִלִּפְנֵי הַקָּדוֹשׁ
6:69	One, blessed be He, to descend and rescue him from the fire of	בָּרוּךְ הוּא לָרֶדֶת לְהַצִּילוֹ מֵאֵשׁ
6:71	Nimrod. And the angel Gabriel came to him and said to him,	נִמְרוֹד. וַיָּבֹא אֵלָיו הַמַּלְאָךְ גַּבְרִיאֵל וַיֹּאמֶר לוֹ,
6:73	"Abraham, should I save you from this fire?"	"מָה אַבְרָהָם אַצִּילְךָ מִזֶּה הָאֵשׁ?"
6:75	Abraham said to him, "The God in whom I trust, the God of	וַיֹּאמֶר לוֹ, "הָאֱלֹהִים אֲשֶׁר אֲנִי בוֹטֵחַ בּוֹ, אֱלֹהֵי
6:77	the heavens and the God of the earth, He will save me."	הַשָּׁמַיִם וֵאלֹהֵי הָאָרֶץ הוּא יְצִילֵנִי."

P'shat: 6:61–62. the God whom you serve. Abraham's mother (despite hearing his words of truth) remains an idolater. As was the case with Nimrod earlier in the midrash, merely hearing the truth is not enough if one stubbornly remains unaffected by it. **6:68. sought mercy.** The angels seek to arouse God's mercy and gain God's permission to descend to earth in order to extinguish Nimrod's fire and save Abraham. **6:71–72. the angel Gabriel came to him.** Gabriel descends to earth to appear before Abraham. **6:75. Abraham said to him.** This illustrates not only the Patriarch's great faith and courage, but also his willingness to speak up before God.

D'rash: 6:59–60. his words that they were true. The text employs the term דִּבְרֵי צַדִּיקִים (*divrei tzadikim*) to indicate "true words." But the term may also mean "righteous things" or even "deeds of the righteous." The midrash teaches that our acts of goodness possess the power to help us transcend the challenges mounted by an idolatrous, materialistic world that threaten to destroy our Judaism. **6:65. launching pad.** The Hebrew כַּף (*kaf*) literally means "palm" or "fist" and implies being in the grasp of something or someone evil. The Redemption (*G'ulah*) section of the Evening Service (directly following the *Sh'ma*) states: "You are our Sovereign: You deliver us from the hand of oppressors, and save us from the fist [כַּף, *kaf*] of tyrants. You do wonders without number, marvels that pass our understanding." In this case, the launching pad is an extension of the fist of the tyrant, Nimrod, who plans to thrust Abraham and his faith into the fiery furnace of destruction. The term כַּף (*kaf*) also bears another connotation, that of the כַּף זְכוּת (*kaf z'chut*), the "scale of merit." The midrash reminds us of God's judgment of our merits on these High Holy Days and teaches that each trial can be either a negative force in our moral and religious lives or an opportunity for merit.

Our behavior in trial can strengthen the impulse for good within us. **6:71–72. the angel Gabriel came to him**. The Babylonian Talmud *(P'sachim)* presents a slightly different version: When the angel Gabriel requests of God that he be permitted to descend and save the righteous Abraham from the fiery furnace, God replies, "I am unique in My world, and he is unique in his world; it is fitting for Him who is unique to deliver him who is unique." But because God does not withhold the merited reward of any creature, Gabriel is awarded the privilege of saving Hananiah, Mishael, and Azariah (the Hebrew names of Shadrach, Meshach, and Abed-Nego) from Nebuchadnezzar's fiery furnace in the future. When the time comes, God orders Gabriel to descend. Gabriel, the Prince of Fire, goes down and performs a "miracle within a miracle." That is, he cools the fire within the furnace, saving the Jews, while at the same time causing the heat and flames to leap outside the furnace and kill those who cast the righteous into the fire. In both versions, that of the Talmud and that found in *Maaseh Avraham Avinu*, God's omnipotence and providence are highlighted. The stories also reflect the import of the trial by fire, which the furnace represents, in the annals of Israel's (and the world's) redemption, as well as the exalted spiritual status of Abraham. This incident can be compared to the final plague (killing of the firstborn) in the story of the Exodus, in that the Torah reports that "God Himself" effected this plague. This is an indication of its importance and of God's personal concern. **6:75. Abraham said to him**. By virtue of our position as God's partners, we, like our forebear, Abraham, are able not only to confess, before God, but to profess as well. Jewish tradition provides the leeway for us to bring our concerns before God and to even question our Senior Partner.

6:79 When the Holy One,	וּכְרָאוֹת הַקָּדוֹשׁ
blessed be He, saw his sincere	בָּרוּךְ הוּא כַּוָּנָתוֹ הַטּוֹבָה
6:81 intention, He turned to him in mercy	פָּנָה אֵלָיו בְּרַחֲמִים
and said to the fire, "Be	וַיֹּאמֶר לָאֵשׁ הַהִיא, "תִּהְיֶה
6:83 cool and tranquil upon my	קָרָה וּשְׁלֵוָה עַל
servant Abraham."	עַבְדִּי אַבְרָהָם".
6:85 The Maggid said that the fire	אָמַר הַמַּגִּיד שֶׁהָאֵשׁ
was extinguished without	נִכְבְּתָה בְּלֹא
6:87 water, and the trees flowered	מַיִם וְהָעֵצִים הֵצִיצוּ צִיץ
and all of them brought forth	וְכוּלָּם הוֹצִיאוּ
6:89 fruit.	פֵּירוֹת.

P'shat: **6:80–81. his sincere intention**. God notes Abraham's sincere loyalty, faith, and courage. Not only has Abraham passed the test for all to see, but the efficacy of prayer and good intentions is thusly illustrated. **6:86–87. extinguished without water**. God's word proves sufficient to extinguish the fire. Water is not required, as it would be of a human being attempting to accomplish a similar task. **6:87. and the trees flowered**. The trees that were burning within the furnace not only become extinguished, but so dramatic is their transformation that they even flower and bring forth fruit.

D'rash: 6:80–81. his sincere intention. The word for intention, כַּוָּנָה *(kavanah),* is the same used to connote the sincerity of prayer. Through this we are taught that God takes note of the sincerity of our prayers. In other words, our sincere prayers have the ability to attract God's attention and arouse the divine mercy. **6:81. He turned to him in mercy**. *P'sikta Rabbati* (44:9), in commenting upon the verse "Return, O Israel, unto the Eternal your God" (Hosea 14:2), teaches that as soon as we harness our good intentions and resolve in our hearts to repent, the intention (repentance) soars up until it stands before God's throne of glory. It has also been said (*P'sikta D'Rav Kahana* 23:8) that our acts of repentance can actually move God from the throne of justice to the throne of mercy. Since the High Holy Days commemorate the events of Creation, our chief metaphor for God during this period focuses upon the Holy One as our Creator, who functions as both parent and ruler. As a ruler, God exercises justice in the world. But, as a parent, God shows us love and mercy. Our Sages teach that God does not desire the punishment of those who miss the mark, but rather that they should repent and change their ways. Our confession and sincere good intentions can bring God to forgive us, allowing us to start the New Year with a clean slate. God's balancing of the attributes of justice and mercy is a model to us. As God forgives us, so may we forgive ourselves and others. **6:82. said to the fire**. This parallels the Book of Genesis which depicts God as creating "the heavens and the earth" by the power of divine statement. **6:86–87. extinguished without water**. This echoes the Ten Plagues upon Egypt, for in that case God also demonstrates God's uniqueness by mastery over nature. Both incidents indicate that when people recognize the power of the Creator, the road to redemption is paved. **6:86–87. without water**. *Seder Eliyahu Rabbah* (chapter 6) presents an alternate version in which God, "in tribute to Abraham's righteousness," causes the day to turn cloudy and brings down a rain of such intensity that Nimrod's men cannot get the fire started in the furnace. **6:87. trees flowered**. This echoes Numbers 17:23, which depicts the budding and bearing fruit of Aaron's wooden rod as indicative of divine chosenness and favor.

6:90 Every tree gave forth its fruit, and	כָּל עֵץ נָתַן פִּרְיוֹ
the furnace returned to being like	וְשָׁב הַכִּבְשָׁן כְּמוֹ
6:92 the palace garden. And the angels	גִּינַת הַמֶּלֶךְ, וְהַמַּלְאָכִים
sat with Abraham in its midst.	יוֹשְׁבִים עִם אַבְרָהָם בְּתוֹכוֹ.
6:94 The king turned and saw the garden,	וַיִּפֶן הַמֶּלֶךְ וַיַּרְא אֶת הַגָּן
and the angels sitting with Abraham	וְאֶת הַמַּלְאָכִים יוֹשְׁבִים עִם
6:96 in the midst of the garden.	אַבְרָהָם בְּתוֹךְ הַגָּן.
The king said to Abraham, "Great	וַיֹּאמֶר הַמֶּלֶךְ לְאַבְרָהָם, "כֶּשֶׁף

6:98 magic. You know that the fire has

no power over you; and at

6:100 the same time, you show the people

that you are sitting in the midst of

6:102 the palace garden."

גָּדוֹל. אַתָּה יוֹדֵעַ שֶׁהָאֵשׁ

אֵינָהּ שׁוֹלֶטֶת בְּךָ, וְלֹא

עוֹד אֶלָּא שֶׁאַתָּה מַרְאֶה לָעָם

שֶׁאַתָּה יוֹשֵׁב בְּתוֹךְ

גִּנַּת בֵּיתָן."

P'shat: **6:90. gave forth its fruit**. Fruit is a symbol of life. **6:91. furnace returned**. Abraham's righteousness coupled with God's power effects this great redemption. The garden, which was transformed by the king into a furnace of death, again returns to its beautiful and pristine state, bursting forth with life. **6:94. The king turned**. In contrast to God, who turns to Abraham in mercy, Nimrod, even after witnessing the great redemption before him, turns to accuse. **6:97–98. Great magic**. The king's sarcastic response communicates that his heart and head remain hard, closed, cynical. Magic is characteristic of idolatry, for in the idolatrous mind-set the gods are beneath nature and therefore can be manipulated by the magician who can control nature. **6:100. you show the people**. The king claims that the divine redemption he has just witnessed is a ruse perpetrated by Abraham to further his own personal agenda.

D'rash: **6:91. furnace returned**. Abraham's "turning" to God in sincere prayer causes God to "turn" to him in mercy, which subsequently causes the component parts of the fiery furnace (natural resources turned to the tasks of destruction) to "return" to their pristine, peaceful state. The path to personal change and society's redemption can begin with the sincerity of our High Holy Day prayer experience. **6:97–98. Great magic**. This parallels *Targum Yonatan* to Genesis 11:28: "When all the people who were there saw that the fire had no power over Abram, they said to themselves, 'Is not Haran, the brother of Abram, full of divination and sorcery? It is he who uttered charms over the fire so that it would not burn his brother.' Immediately, fire fell from the heavens on high and consumed him, and Haran died in sight of his father." The allusion to magic also proves reminiscent of the Pharaohs of Egypt, who rely upon magicians, as opposed to recognizing the One God. The faith of the Jewish people, on the other hand, is summed up by the observations of Balaam, the prophet to the nations: "For there is no divination in Jacob and no magic in Israel. Even now it is said to Jacob and Israel what God has wrought" (Numbers 23:23). **6:100. you show the people**. Dishonest people often suspect others of dishonesty, for they assume that everyone believes and behaves as they do. In this case, Nimrod, who perverted religion and masqueraded behind the power of Adam's garment (originally made by God for Adam and inherited by Nimrod; animals would bow down before it) to further his own ambitions and consolidate his rulership, suspects Abraham of perpetrating the same. As opposed to Nimrod's attitude, we read in *Pirkei Avot* the teaching of Y'hoshua ben P'rachyah that one should "judge everyone favorably." That is, everyone should be given the benefit of the doubt.

6:103 All the ministers of	וַיַּעֲנוּ כָּל שָׂרֵי
Nimrod answered to the king in unison,	נִמְרוֹד יַחְדָּיו לַמֶּלֶךְ,
6:105 "No, our lord. This	"לֹא אֲדוֹנֵינוּ אֵין
is not magic. But rather, the	זֶה כִּשּׁוּף כִּי אִם
6:107 ability of a great God, the God	יְכֹלֶת אֱלוֹהַ גָּדוֹל, אֱלֹהֵי
of Abraham. And there is no	אַבְרָהָם וְאֵין
6:109 other God besides Him.	אֱלוֹהַ אַחֵר בִּלְבָדוֹ.
And we attest to this, and also that	וַאֲנַחְנוּ מְעִידִים עַל זֶה וְגַם
6:111 Abraham is His true servant."	אַבְרָהָם עַבְדּוֹ בֶּאֱמֶת."
And at that moment, all the	וַיַּאֲמִינוּ בְּשָׁעָה הַהִיא כָּל
6:113 ministers of Nimrod and all	שָׂרֵי נִמְרוֹד וְכָל
his people believed in the	עַמּוֹ
6:115 Eternal, the God of Abraham;	בַּיי אֱלֹהֵי אַבְרָהָם
and they all said,	וַיֹּאמְרוּ כּוּלָם,
6:117 "The Eternal, He is God in the	"יי הוּא הָאֱלֹהִים
heavens above and on the earth	בַּשָּׁמַיִם מִמַּעַל וְעַל הָאָרֶץ
6:119 below; there is none other!"	מִתַּחַת אֵין עוֹד!"

P'shat: 6:105–106. This is not magic. Unlike the close-minded Nimrod, his ministers and his people are moved to recognize the truth about God. **6:110. we attest.** This is the attestation that Abraham predicts earlier in the midrash. **6:113–114. all his people believed.** The tables have turned not only vis-à-vis the fiery furnace itself, but in the general pattern of God's influence as well. At the beginning of *Maaseh Avraham Avinu*, only one person professed belief in the Eternal, His servant Abraham. Now, upon the midrash's conclusion, there exists only one person who won't attest to God's greatness in the heavens and the earth, the idolatrous Nimrod.

D'rash: 6:117–119. The Eternal, He is God ... there is none other. The midrash concludes as do many other episodes in the sacred history of our people—with a doxology, an unadulterated praise of God. Thus, the ending of *Maaseh Avraham Avinu* resembles that of the story of Elijah the prophet versus the priests of Baal. In both instances, everyone freely proclaims the Eternal as God. The Exodus from Egypt also ends with praise of God, as we read in the Song of the Sea, "The Eternal will reign for ever and ever" (Exodus 15:18). This pattern is discernible in the Pesach Haggadah as well, which leads us through the experience "from ignominy to praise" (מִגְּנוּת לְשֶׁבַח, *mignut l'shevach*). That is, we go from the bitterness of slavery to the praise of God. *Maaseh Avraham Avinu* may also be thought to follow a similar trajectory: from the disgrace of idolatry (spiritual slavery) to the praise of the Holy One (spiritual glory). In the Book of Daniel, Nebuchadnezzar addresses the gathering round the fiery furnace subsequent to the rescue of the three Jews, saying, "Blessed be the God of Shadrach, Meshach, and Abed-Nego, who has sent His angel, and delivered His servants that trusted in Him, and have changed the king's word. He has yielded their bodies that they might not serve nor worship any god except their own God" (Daniel 3:28). By the end of *Maaseh Avraham Avinu*, everyone, except the evil Nimrod, recognizes the legitimacy of worshiping the One God, as well as the Eternal's power to redeem.

GLEANINGS

Trials Inflicted

Ten trials were inflicted upon Abraham,
and he withstood them all.
Why?
To show how great was his commitment.

Suffering is the stuff of life,
and through suffering
one opens the heart to compassion,
the shared pain of living beings.

We withstand our trials
by feeling the pain without abandoning the
    world.

Suffering without bitterness,
we do justly, even in the face of unjust adversity.

Rami M. Shapiro, *Wisdom of the Jewish Sages*
(New York: Bell Tower, 1993), page 101

Abraham's Achievement

This model of Abraham's achievement represents a fragile equilibrium; on the one side, worldliness, on the other, madness. It is the awareness of this tension that characterizes Abraham's "reeling" motion. Current explanations of the world no longer work for him; the *shogeh* [שׁוֹגֶה]—alienation caused by "love of righteousness"—contains within it (in the English word, as well as in the Hebrew— alienation was one of the clinical terms for madness) both hazard and the birth of a "terrible beauty."

Avivah Gottlieb Zornberg, *The Beginning of Desire: Reflections on Genesis* (New York: Image Books, 1995), page 89

Pleasure in Repentance

Both asking and granting forgiveness therefore demand considerable strength of character.

It matters therefore that God is portrayed as one "who takes pleasure in repentance," because at stake is a fundamental tenet of Jewish theology: God is not mean or vindictive; God has standards, but deals compassionately with those who do not meet them, as long as they honestly try to return to the right path. God's compassion enables us to make amends, to get past wrongdoing, and to get on with our lives. We need not remain stuck in the disabling guilt and the despair of sin.

Elliot Dorff, in *My People's Prayer Book: Traditional Prayers, Modern Commentaries*, vol. 2, *The Amidah*, ed. Lawrence Hoffman (Woodstock, Vt.: Jewish Lights, 1998), page 105

Another Version

Terach took Abram and handed him over to Nimrod. Nimrod said to Abram, "Let us bow down to fire." "If so," said Abram, "shall we bow down to water, which extinguishes fire?" "Let us bow down to water," Nimrod responded. "If so," said Abram, "shall we bow down to the clouds, which carry water?" "Let us bow down to the clouds," Nimrod responded. "If so," said Abram, "shall we bow down to the wind, which scatters the clouds?" "Let us bow down to the wind," responded Nimrod. "And shall we bow down to man, who contains the wind?" asked Abram. Nimrod said, "Why do you speak so much? I bow down only to fire. Now I shall throw you into it, and let the God to whom you bow come and save you." Abram descended into the fiery furnace and was saved.

B'reishit Rabbah 38:13

God's Mercy Aroused

Abraham was bent, bound, and placed on the floor. Then they surrounded him with five cubits of wood on all four sides. Until then, Terach had not recognized his Creator. The neighbors and townspeople came, banged Terach on the head, and said to him, "For shame! The one whom you said would inherit this world and the world-to-come will be burned in Nimrod's fire." Thereupon God's mercy was aroused, and He descended and saved Abraham.

Yalkut Shimoni, Lech L'cha 77

Delicious Fruits

He planted an orchard with all species of delicious fruits. According to one Sage, he built an inn, and he caused God's name to be called by every passerby. How? After they ate and drank, they would want to bless Abraham. He would say to them, "Did you eat food that belongs to me? You ate that which is God's. Thank, praise, and bless the One who spoke and the world came to be."

Babylonian Talmud, *Sotah* 10b

And God Tested Abraham

Another name for this day is *Yom ha Din*, the day of judgment. Surely, Abraham was judged on this day. And tradition teaches us that we are all judged on this day. . . . We must judge ourselves. That is the essence of *t'shuvah*, this time of turning. . . . The beginning of wisdom is the ability to know oneself, and to judge oneself. And once we know how to judge ourselves, to save ourselves, we can become among those who save others.

Sue Levi Elwell, "Rosh Hashanah Sermon 1987,"
in *Four Centuries of Jewish Women's Spirituality,*
ed. Ellen M. Umansky and Dianne Ashton
(Boston: Beacon Press, 1992), page 270

Justice and Compassion

In Hebrew, the words "justice" and "compassion" are expressed by a single word, *tsadakah,* which implies that true justice must always be mingled with compassion. Justice without compassion is heartless; compassion without justice has no moral authority.

Naomi H. Rosenblatt and Joshua Horwitz, *Wrestling with*
Angels (New York: Delta, 1995), page 170

Abraham: A Part of Us

Abraham is that part of us that asks: What does a life *mean*? What—after all the acquisitions, mergers, promotions, and deals—*matters*? What gives us the deepest sense of significance, value, and purpose in our life? For these questions Abraham is the Western tradition's first guide and emissary. When we ask these questions, we enter an inscape of thought and feeling, and he was there before us.

Peter Pitzele, *Our Fathers' Wells: A Personal Encounter*
with the Myths of Genesis (San Francisco: Harper
San Francisco, 1995), page 84

The Sanctification of God's Name

Concerning the system of commandments, the Torah instructs that we are to "live by them" (Leviticus 18:5). The Rabbis interpret this to mean that the mitzvot were revealed to promote life, that we may live by them, and not die by them. That is, any mitzvah may be pushed aside for the sake of saving a life or even if there is a chance that life may be risked.

There are, however, three exceptions to the above rule. The Talmud teaches that we should sacrifice our own life rather than commit murder, adultery, or idolatry. Murder is never permitted, the Talmud reasons, for this would mean the death of another human being, an equal who was created *b'tzelem elohim,* in God's image. As it is written in the Talmud, "And who is to say that your blood is redder than his?" (Babylonian Talmud, *Sanhedrin* 61b). To transgress by means of adultery would mean the death of the family, terminating relationships brought together and sanctified in God's presence. Finally, it is better to give up our life, as a sacrifice, for the "sanctification of God's name" (עַל קִדּוּשׁ הַשֵּׁם, *al kiddush HaShem*) rather than commit idolatry, for the practice of idolatry would mean the death of Judaism, and thus the destruction of the Jewish people.

Yet, for a death to serve as a sanctification of God's name, certain conditions must be met. First, the idolatry must be public; that is, a minyan, ten Jewish adults, must be present. If the sin of idolatry is not known publicly, the transgression doesn't affect God's position in the eyes of others. Second, the nature of the activity itself must be of such a type that it serves no obvious material benefit to the oppressor. If Nimrod would have forced Abraham, under threat of death, to mow the royal lawn on Shabbat, Jewish law would provide for Abraham to have cut the grass and save his life, since anyone watching would not have assumed Judaism to be patently false or a laughingstock. Rather, people would have only surmised that the king really wanted his grounds manicured! Since, however, Nimrod insisted Abraham bow down to him in worship, a move that would have indicated to the newly converted surrounding crowd the falsehood of Judaism, Abraham chose to resist, at the possible cost of his life for the sanctification of God's name. Thus, by his willingness to give up his life in the episode of the fiery furnace, Abraham was putting himself on the line in order to safeguard the spiritual gains he had brought to the world.

This raises the question of how we, in our lives, safeguard Judaism. It is wise to take heed of Abraham's example. He not only preached the truth, but was willing to put his own life on the line for the Jewish people. By his actions, Abraham demonstrated belief in God and the kindness to others that such faith demands. Abraham taught righteousness to his son, and the rest of his spiritual progeny as well, by modeling the correct behaviors.

And so must we. If we are to safeguard Judaism, we must do so actively. In order to promote God's presence of morality and kindness in the world, we must do so by the strength of our actions. If our children are to follow in our footsteps, we ourselves must take the first steps. In this midrash, Abraham displayed the courage and conviction to stand up for what was right amidst an idolatrous world. He is our role model in faith, goodness, self-growth, and humility. May we, as God's partners, seek to emulate his example.

Postscript: A Rabbinic Response to the Challenges of Jewish Survival

In addition to its function as a preparation for and a companion piece to the High Holy Days, *Maaseh Avraham Avinu* may also be seen as a rabbinic response to the challenges of Jewish survival. In considering the midrash in this light, the character of Nimrod represents more than just the personage we encounter in chapter 10 of the Book of Genesis. Rather, to the rabbinic mind, Nimrod symbolizes those who have placed themselves above God's law, all those tyrants throughout history who oppressed and would have destroyed the Jewish people; while Abraham, on the other hand, symbolizes Jewish adherence to faith, Torah, and God's commandments.

Significantly, as the midrash relates how God saves Abraham from the flames of Nimrod's fire, it offers the hope that God will save the Jewish people from the destruction of their latter-day persecutors. Thus, the redemption of Abraham and its parallel, the Exodus from Egypt, serve as models for the redemption of the future. This optimistic vision of the future is further symbolized in the midrash by God's turning the raging furnace back into a garden, bearing the fruits of life and peace. Upon its conclusion, then, *Maaseh Avraham Avinu* leaves us with an image of the "end of days" akin to the turning of spears into pruning hooks, all sitting beneath their trees with none to make them afraid, a return to the pristine state of the Garden of Eden.

That human beings possess the power to increase God's influence for good in the world stands out as another of the midrash's lessons appropriate to the issues of Jewish survival. Just as in the midrash Nimrod's tyrannical power in the world is diminished in direct proportion to the number of people who attest to God in their lives, so too does the religious commitment of every Jew help defeat the power of evil in the world. It is not Abraham's military prowess or propensity to violence that scatters Nimrod's army. Rather, the dense cloud of God's Torah and providence repels their brute savagery. It is the "living water," another metaphor for Torah, that saves Abraham's life while imprisoned without food or drink. The midrash then imparts a strategy for Jewish survival in its teaching that our dedication to Torah, and the righteousness and providence that stem from it, constitute the most important weapons in turning the tide against the savage persecutors of this world.

And not only is this the path to mere survival for its own sake, but spreading God's message of righteousness constitutes the fulfillment of Israel's destiny. Just as Abraham, in the midrash, is purposefully "created" (נִבְרָה, *nivrah*) by God, so too is the Jewish people created and chosen by God for a purpose, a mission. The text depicts Abraham's divinely ordained mission as defeating evil by spreading God's goodness; so too is this the task of his descendants.

Hence, *Maaseh Avraham Avinu* places the suffering of the Jewish people into this larger context of purpose and mission. The midrashic tradition teaches that God tested Abraham, making him undergo a series of trials and sufferings, in order to refine his character and hold him up as a positive example to the world. This is what it means to be God's servant. The Jewish people, as God's servants, can expect to be tried. To act as God's devoted representative is no easy task. It may well involve pain and persecution, such as the suffering Abraham endured at the hand of Nimrod. Being God's servant may also involve resisting the types of temptations posed by Satan and Abraham's mother in the midrash. These pressures may take many forms and project varied voices. Under the guise of "what's in it for me?," "go with the flow; everyone else is," or "consider your career," these influences often seduce us to abandon our most cherished principles, our higher selves, our very Jewishness.

Yet, despite all the troubles of this world, the evil, the violence, the idolatry, and the unjust persecutions, the midrash ends on a note of hope. Acting as God's servants, serving God's purpose may not be easy, but it is necessary and ultimately rewarding. Our efforts can and will make a difference in this world. Our prayers are heard. God is watching us. Divine justice is continually operative. Our suffering has meaning. Someday goodness will prevail and peace will be achieved in the end.

Glossary

Akeidah—Literally, "binding"; the term traditionally refers to the story of Abraham's intended sacrifice of his son Isaac, as told in Genesis, chapter 22. The biblical text relates God's commanding Abraham to "take him up," father and son ascending Mount Moriah together, Abraham's binding of Isaac upon the altar, and the last-minute divine intervention that prevents the sacrifice's consummation. Genesis 22 is one of the Torah readings designated for Rosh HaShanah.

Aleinu—Ancient prayer, originally composed for the Shofar Service of Rosh HaShanah. Since the Middle Ages, it has been included in every worship service. The prayer begins with our obligation to praise "the God of all" through bowing and prostration. It continues to express the hope that God will help us heal the world so that the day may come when "You shall be One and Your name shall be One," that is, all humanity shall live by the basic tenets of God's morality.

al kiddush HaShem—Literally, "for the sanctification of God's name"; this expression refers to martyrdom for the sake of God, Judaism, and the Jewish people.

Amidah—see **T'filah**.

Amora—Talmudic Rabbi. The period of the *Amoraim* extends from about 220 C.E. to approximately 500 C.E.

Aseret Y'mei T'shuvah—Literally, the "Ten Days of Return"; the term refers to the High Holy Day period that encompasses the ten days from Rosh HaShanah to Yom Kippur, the first through the tenth of the Hebrew month Tishrei. *T'shuvah* ("repentance" or "returning" to God's right path) is one of the major themes and goals of these days, hence the appellation.

Avot D'Rabbi Natan—Compiled by Rabbi Natan the Babylonian, a second-century-C.E. contemporary of Rabbi Meir. The text consists of a series of *baraitot,* tannaitic material outside of the Mishnah, which interpret and midrashically expand upon the Mishnaic tractate concerning ethical behavior, *Avot* (often referred to as *Pirkei Avot,* or Chapters of the Ancestors).

B.C.E.—An abbreviation denoting "before the Common Era." This designation is used for years before the year 0. This is the same period that is described by B.C., "before Christ," used in reference to years before the birth of Jesus. Since the notion of Jesus' deification is not consonant with Jewish theology, many Jews have adhered to the use of B.C.E.

B'midbar Rabbah—Exegetic midrash on the Book of Numbers compiled in the twelfth century C.E. Scholars attribute the midrash to the school of Moshe HaDarshan, a medieval biblical commentator who taught in Narbonne, France.

B'reishit Rabbah—Aggadic midrash on the Book of Genesis written down in the fifth century C.E., but containing earlier tannaitic material. The work incorporates 100 sections, each headed by a quotation from Genesis leading to a chain of interpretive *aggadot.*

C.E.—An abbreviation denoting "the Common Era." This designation is used for years since the year 0. This is the same period that is described by A.D. or *anno Domini*, Latin for "in the year of our Lord," used in reference to years elapsed since the birth of Jesus. Since the notion of Jesus' deification is not consonant with Jewish theology, many Jews have adhered to the use of C.E.

cheshbon hanefesh—Literally, an "accounting of the soul"; this activity is seen as a vital step in the process of *t'shuvah* and, hence, essential to the Days of Awe.

chutzpadik—A Yiddishism derived from the Hebrew *chutzpah,* indicating someone or something that is characterized by insolence, and/or nerve.

Days of Awe—The name given to the ten-day period from Rosh HaShanah through Yom Kippur. This period is also known as the Ten Days of Repentance.

Eichah Rabbah—Midrashic collection on the Book of Lamentations. The work is divided into two parts. The first is a series of *proems,* or homiletic introductions. The second part is an exegetic midrash on the text of Lamentations. One of the most ancient of midrashim, the work was probably written down in the fourth or fifth century C.E.

Gates of Repentance—The name of the official *machzor* (High Holy Day prayer book) of the Reform Movement. Originally published in 1978 by the Central Conference of American Rabbis, the text was revised in 1996 by Rabbi Chaim Stern to reflect gender sensitivity.

g'matria—A type of numerology in which the numerical equivalents of the Hebrew letters are tallied to provide another level of interpretation.

g'zeirah shavah—A hermeneutic principle by which the Torah is interpreted through the presence of identical words and/or terms found in two or more passages.

High Holy Days—The common appellation given to Rosh HaShanah and Yom Kippur, the New Year and the Day of Atonement.

K'dushat HaYom—Literally, "the Holiness of the Day"; the section of the Holy Day *T'filah* that is specifically geared to the special day being observed. It takes the place of the thirteen requests that usually comprise the middle section of the weekday *T'filah.*

leitvort—German for "lead word"; the term points to a word in a biblical passage that runs throughout and thus communicates a major theme. Martin Buber, a twentieth-century commentator, championed the concept of the *leitvort*.

Magid—The "storytelling" section of the Pesach seder. Also the term used to refer to the narrator or "storyteller" in *Maaseh Avraham Avinu* (spelled as "Maggid" in the body of the text). The word may also mean "preacher."

Maimonides—Also known by the acronym Rambam, Maimonides was born in Spain in 1135. After leaving the country of his birth, Maimonides traveled to Palestine and eventually settled in Egypt, where he lived until his death in 1204. He wrote extensively on Jewish law and philosophy. He is best known for his code, the *Mishneh Torah,* and his philosophic treatise, *Guide for the Perplexed.*

midrash—From the Hebrew verb *lidrosh,* to "extract" or "search out"; midrash is that class of rabbinic literature that seeks to find contemporary meaning in biblical text by filling in between the lines of Scripture.

Midrash HaGadol—A thirteenth-century midrashic anthology on the Torah emanating from Yemen. Compiled by David ben Amram Adani, it consists mainly of excerpts of older rabbinic texts of the tannaitic and amoraic periods.

Midrash T'hillim—Exegetic midrash on Psalms set down in the tenth century C.E., also known as *Midrash Shocheir Tov.*

Mishnah—The compilation of Oral Torah explicating the laws of the Five Books of Moses, edited by Rabbi Y'hudah HaNasi in the year 200 C.E. The Mishnah and the Gemara, which helps explain the former, comprise the Talmud.

Mishnah Yoma—The tractate of the Mishnah that deals with the laws of Yom Kippur. The designation *Yoma,* Aramaic for "The Day," communicates the awesome character and great import of the Day of Atonement.

mitzvah—A divine commandment, a religious obligation; also used colloquially to indicate a good deed.

Nazarite—A religious devotee who vowed to withdraw from intoxicating liquors, grape products, cutting of hair, and ritual defilements (especially contact with the dead), as described in Numbers, chapter 6. The Bible reports of two children who were dedicated as Nazirites from before birth and remained so throughout their lives, Samson and Samuel.

N'ilah—Literally, "the Closing"; the *N'ilah* service is the final rubric of worship on Yom Kippur. As such it represents the "closing of the gates" for the High Holy Day period.

Pirkei Avot—Literally, "Chapters of the Ancestors"; the tractate of the Mishnah that deals exclusively with the tenets of ethical behavior as set down by the Sages from the third century B.C.E. to the third century C.E.

Pirkei D'Rabbi Eliezer—Tannaitic midrash on Genesis and the first chapters of Exodus. The work is traditionally ascribed to first-century-C.E. teacher Rabbi Eliezer ben Hyrcanus, hence the title.

piyut—From the Greek *poites*, the term refers to a form of Hebrew liturgical poem. *Piyutim* are added to the Jewish worship services of the various holy days of the year as an enhancement. The *Un'taneh Tokef,* a *piyut* that declares the awesome power of the High Holy Days, embedded within the Rosh HaShanah and Yom Kippur *T'filah,* is one of the most distinctive prayers of the Days of Awe.

P'sikta D'Rav Kahana—A collection of thirty-two midrashic homilies (early rabbinic sermons) for the Festivals and special Sabbaths of the year. The work was probably written down in the seventh century C.E., but contains earlier material. Rav Kahana of the title is thought to be either the third-century-C.E. *Amora,* a disciple of Rav, or a *Gaon* (post-talmudic Babylonian spiritual leader) of the same name.

P'sikta Rabbati—A collection of forty-eight midrashic homilies for the festivals and special Sabbaths of the year. Although similar in format to *P'sikta D'Rav Kahana, P'sikta Rabbati* is of later origin, having been compiled around the ninth century C.E.

Rashi—Acronym for Rabbi Shlomo Yitzchaki, medieval scholar (1040–1105 C.E.) who lived in Troyes, France. Rashi is famous for his commentaries to the Torah and Talmud.

Rav—Also known as Abba the Tall because of his great stature, Rav was an early-third-century-C.E. Babylonian *Amora.* Born in Kafri, Babylonia, he traveled to Palestine to study with his uncle, Rabbi Chiya, and with Rabbi Y'hudah HaNasi. Upon returning to Babylonia, Rav established the academy at Sura. Rav's school, along with the academy at Nehardiya, headed by Rav's colleague, Shmuel, became a leading educational institution in the Jewish world, boasting over 1,200 students. The teachings of Rav and Shmuel figure prominently in the Babylonian Talmud.

Ruth Rabbah—Exegetic midrash on the Book of Ruth, written down in the sixth century C.E., but containing earlier material.

Sefer HaYashar—Early-twelfth-century aggadic work, containing earlier midrashic material. The book is written in narrative form and arranged according to the weekly Torah readings, along with sections reflecting the Books of Joshua and Judges. The work covers the history of humankind from the creation of Adam to the period of the judges and includes a version of the stories of Nimrod, Terach, and Abraham.

Sefer Rokeach—Thirteenth-century guide to ethics and halachah (Jewish law) written by Rabbi Elazar ben Y'hudah of Worms, Germany.

S'fat Emet—Discourses on the Torah and other subjects written by the Chasidic master Rabbi Y'hudah Leib Alter (1847–1905). Alter was the second rebbe of Ger and a leader of Polish Jewry.

Sforno—Popular appellation assigned to Rabbi Ovadyah ben Yaakov Sforno (1475–1550). Rabbi Ovadyah lived most of his life in Bologna, Italy, where he practiced medicine, conducted a yeshiva, and wrote classic commentaries to the Torah and *Pirkei Avot*. Sforno's commentaries generally seek to elucidate the *p'shat,* the plain meaning of the text.

Shevet Musar—A homiletic discourse on ethics compiled by Elijah HaCohen of Smyrna, Turkey, and originally published in Amsterdam in 1732. The book is divided into fifty-two chapters, each extolling a particular ethical virtue. *Maaseh Avraham Avinu* comprises more than half of the book's final chapter, concerning the virtue of humility.

Sh'ma—Ancient rubric of worship taken from Deuteronomy 6:4, "Hear, O Israel: the Eternal is our God, the Eternal is One." In Hebrew, the first word is *Sh'ma,* hence the title.

Sh'mot Rabbah—Aggadic midrash on the Book of Exodus written down in the tenth or eleventh century C.E., but containing earlier materials.

S'lichot—Literally, "Penitential Prayers"; the term has also come to refer to special penitential services offered in preparation for the High Holy Days. In the Sephardic tradition, these services take place each morning of Elul (the month preceding the New Year) prior to the Morning Service. Ashkenazim begin *S'lichot* services during the week preceding Rosh HaShanah. The first of these generally occurs late-night on the Saturday evening preceding the High Holy Days (provided it falls at least four days before Rosh HaShanah; otherwise *S'lichot* begins on the previous Saturday evening).

Talmud—Vast collection of rabbinic law and lore, the Talmud consists of two parts: the Mishnah, which seeks to interpret the Torah, and the Gemara, which seeks to "complete" the Mishnah by explaining what it really means. The Talmud appears in two versions: the more extensive "Babylonian Talmud," a collection of discussions by the rabbis of Babylonia from the second to fifth centuries C.E., and the smaller "Jerusalem Talmud" (also known as the "Palestinian Talmud"), compiled by the Rabbis of the Land of Israel from the second to fourth centuries C.E.

Tanna—Mishnaic Rabbi. The period of the *Tannaim* extends from approximately 100 B.C.E. to about 220 C.E.

Tanna D'Vei Eliyahu—Aggadic midrash, also known as *Seder Eliyahu.* Scholars disagree as to the work's authorship and place of origin. Most agree, however, that the midrash was probably written down in the seventh century C.E. The midrash is divided into two parts: *Seder Eliyahu Rabbah* (The Major Order of Eliyahu) and *Seder Eliyahu Zuta* (The Minor Order of Eliyahu).

Targum—Literally, "translation"; the term usually refers to the translation of the Torah into Aramaic by Onkelos, a first-century-C.E. student of Rabbi Akiva. The *Targum* is considered to be an authoritative interpretation of Scripture that attempts to communicate the straightforward meaning of the text. It is frequently referred to by Rashi and other major commentators.

Targum Yonatan—Interpretive translation of the Torah into Aramaic reputedly written by Yonatan ben Uziel, a disciple of Hillel (first century B.C.E.).

Taryag Mitzvot—Term used to refer to all 613 commandments revealed in the Torah. While mitzvot is Hebrew for "commandments," *taryag* is an acronym derived from the Hebrew letter equivalents to 613 (תרי"ג).

T'filah—Literally, "Prayer"; the Rabbis use this as a technical term indicating the *Amidah* or "Standing Prayer." It is the central rabbinic text of the Jewish worship service. While the first three and the final three blessings remain constant (although they are expanded for the High Holy Days), the middle section changes to accommodate the day.

Tikkun Leil Rosh HaShanah—A selection of holy text(s) to be studied on the evening of the Jewish New Year, designed to properly inculcate the mood and values of the High Holy Day season. The scribe of the Valmadonna Trust manuscript 167 edition of *Maaseh Avraham Avinu* wrote that the midrash should be recited on the first evening of the New Year as a *Tikkun Leil Rosh HaShanah*.

tikkun olam—Literally, "healing the world"; the term refers to the activities involved in fixing those aspects of the world and society that constitute obstacles to the bringing of a messianic age to humankind.

Torah—Literally, "Teaching"; the name given to the Five Books of Moses, the first five books of the Bible, the source book of Judaism. Sometimes the appellation is used to describe the entire enterprise of Jewish holy learning.

Tosefta—Collection of tannaitic materials that were left out of the Mishnah. Traditionally thought to be edited by Rabbi Chiya and his circle around 220 C.E., the *Tosefta* functions as a parallel to and an expansion upon the Mishnah.

t'shuvah—Frequently translated as "repentance," the Hebrew literally means "turning." As such, *t'shuvah* represents our turning away from sin, and returning to God and to a higher vision of ourselves. The call to *t'shuvah* is one of the major themes of the High Holy Days, as the liturgy asserts, *"T'shuvah,* prayer, and *tzedakah* temper judgment's severe decree." See **Aseret Y'mei T'shuvah**.

tzedakah—Literally, "righteousness"; the term is often used to indicate our obligations to help others, particularly the poor.

Tz'einah U'R'einah—Yiddish paraphrase and interpretation of the Torah consisting of rabbinic commentaries and legends. It was written by Yaakov ben Yitzchak Ashkenazi of Yanof in 1618 as an educational tract for women. The title, meaning "Go Forth and See," is taken from Song of Songs 3:11, "Go forth and see, you daughters of Zion."

Yalkut Shimoni—A thirteenth-century midrashic anthology covering the entire Bible, attributed to Shimon HaDarshan of Frankfurt-on-Mein. It is the best known and most comprehensive of the midrashic anthologies. The anthology preserves many sections from midrashic works no longer extant.

Zohar—The Hebrew title for the "Book of Splendor," the thirteenth-century classic of Jewish mysticism.